Praise for

my pursuit of beauty

"*Dynasty*, produced by my dad, Aaron Spelling, sparked the imagination of my friend Vince Spinnato and inspired him to turn his dreams of developing luxury beauty products into a reality. His no-holds-barred memoir describing his struggles to the top is brutally honest, hilarious, and heartbreaking. I couldn't put the book down."

—Tori Spelling
Actress, Producer, and Author of *sTori Telling*,
Mommywood, and more

"I met Vince through my makeup artist and best friend in London, Jo Sugar, who raved about not only his products, but his passion. Being a product junkie myself, I told her to give him my number, which has led into a wonderful journey of his skin care lines. His honesty and his scientific talent about the skincare industry have made me love this book and his products. Growing up with the legendary iconic faces of MGM royalty like my mother, Judy Garland, I understand the trust you need to have in today's confusing billion-dollar beauty industry. When you find the right 'wizard,' you are grateful and stay connected."

—Lorna Luft
Singer, Actress, *New York Times*–Bestselling Author of
A Star Is Born: Judy Garland and the Film that Got Away, and
Five-Time Emmy Award–Winning Producer of
the Miniseries *Life with Judy Garland: Me and My Shadows*

"As a beauty professional and founder of the largest 'meeting and discussing' book club in the world, I knew from the first chapter that this was a book from the perspective of creating 'beauty' that I had not heard before in a world of reading. Vince Spinnato has a big and real story. I flew through the pages, and oftentimes I was literally on the edge of my velvet-covered seat. What a story! It gets Five Diamonds in the Pulpwood Queen Recommended Reading List. In fact, this dazzling gem of a book is now our Official 2021 February Pulpwood Queen Book Club Selection!"

—Kathy L. Murphy
Artist, Founder of the Pulpwood Queens and Timber Guys Book
Clubs, Author of *The Pulpwood Queens' Tiara Wearing, Book Sharing Guide
to Life*, and Director of Acquisitions of Lucid House Publishing

my pursuit

of

beauty

my pursuit

of

beauty

A COSMETIC CHEMIST REVEALS THE GLITZ, THE GLAM, AND THE BATSH*T CRAZY

VINCE SPINNATO

IN COLLABORATION WITH MICKEY GOODMAN

BOOKLOGIX˙
Alpharetta, GA

The author has tried to recreate events, locations, and conversations from his memories of them. In some instances, in order to maintain their anonymity, the author has changed the names of individuals, companies, and places. He may also have changed some identifying characteristics and details such as physical attributes, occupations, and places of residence.

ISBN: 978-1-61005-964-0 - Paperback
eISBN: 978-1-61005-965-7 - ePub
eISBN: 978-1-61005-966-4 - mobi

Library of Congress Control Number: 2020912285

Printed in the United States of America   1 0 2 7 2 0

⊗ This paper meets the requirements of ANSI/NISO Z39.48-1992 (Permanence of Paper)

*To my mother, father, Grandmother and Grandfather Serra,
sister Teri, and nephew Nicky. Thank you for always supporting
my ambitions and dreams, no matter how crazy they seemed.*

Beauty comes from within . . . jars, bottles, and tubes.
—Anonymous

Contents

Foreword

Vince made a lasting impression on me the very first time we met when he confided that a client of his had asked him to replicate my formula for LipSense®, my company's signature product. He said he had disassociated with her because he didn't want to begin his career by doing something unethical, and that he had heard only good things about me and only terrible things about his client.

We didn't reconnect until years later, when he bounced into my office unannounced and told me that he was working on industry trends. He suggested that my formulas and colors needed revamping. Of course, he knew the perfect cosmetic chemist to do the job—who else but Vince Spinnato?

I could have kicked him out, but his assessment was spot on. So, I laughed out loud and hired him on the spot. It was the beginning of a beautiful collaboration and friendship.

The more we got to know one another, the more I realized that Vince is not only a brilliant chemist, he also has a loving heart and beautiful soul. Vince has his own way to approach and solve thorny problems by finding unique, creative solutions. I treasure his honesty, his loyalty, and his friendship.

He brings that same sense of honesty and openness in this book, taking readers on his bumpy roller-coaster ride through the highs and lows of his life and the beauty industry. Brutally honest and irreverent, it will keep you turning page after page as you traverse his crazy journey. Readers won't be able to put this book down!

Joni Rogers-Kante
Owner and Founder of SeneGence International ®

Preface

My name is Vince Spinnato, and my entire life I've been searching for beauty—in the skincare industry, in my outward appearance, and within myself. From my earliest memories, I felt out of place in my own skin and wanted to be like everybody else. But, it never seemed to work out that way.

To truly understand my journey, I need to first take you back to my upbringing, through my family's neuroses, my torments, adversities, obsessions, phobias, and lovers. Each played a significant part. Only in knowing my past will you be able to understand my present.

Dubai or Bust

I t was a scorching September day in Los Angeles when I got
on the first of several flights that would take me to an important beauty trade show in Dubai. My boss, a jerk and owner
of a natural cosmetic company whose products sold in stores like
Whole Foods and Trader Joe's, insisted that I go, and I sure had
no problem with that. This was, after all, the big time. The show
was the only business event dedicated to the beauty industry in
Dubai. And, yes, Dubai *has* a beauty industry. It's a much larger
market than you might think.

The show draws in thousands of people: distributors, whole-
salers, retailers, salon owners, hair stylists, makeup artists, buyers,
and sellers, like me. We all go to see the latest vibrant, posh, and

over-the-top trends. For me, the trade-show floor is my world—a world of beauty.

On top of all of the glitz and glamour, I wanted to make a splash with my boss. I wanted him to wake up and smell the perfume. He needed to recognize the strides I was making for his budding beauty empire. My goal was to bring back a crap-ton of orders, and then he'd see.

It was a God-awful early flight. My eyes were barely open inside the airport. On top of being exhausted, there was something wrong with the overhead televisions at the gate, and I couldn't even watch the news. But, tired or not, I had an event to attend, and I wasn't going to miss it. For me, the show must go on!

The first leg of my flight was to take me to JFK, but an hour into it, the captain's voice came on the overhead speaker to tell us that we had been diverted to Phoenix. Hell, I was practically still asleep at that God-forsaken hour of the morning. "Phoenix? Is that what he said? Shit!" I said. "Why are we going to Phoenix?"

Passengers began to grumble like a bunch of little old ladies who had come for high tea only to find it had been served cold. We were upset and wanted someone to blame.

Once the plane touched down in Arizona, the captain came on the speaker again. This time, we found out that we couldn't get on another plane to take us the rest of the way to JFK. Odd, but he wouldn't give us any more details. We didn't know why we couldn't fly; we just couldn't.

We were told to get off the plane onto the tarmac. Can you believe that? And damn, even at seven in the morning, it's freaking hot in Phoenix. They then told us to walk into the terminal.

Inside, every television screen was black, reminding me of the airport TVs back in LA. Why were the TVs broken here, too? Did all of these airports use the same cable company or something? Unsettled by the weirdly quiet atmosphere of the airport, I shook my head and refocused.

The airline had definitely screwed the pooch on this one, and I was exceedingly angry. Why wouldn't I be? I was an up-and-comer in the beauty industry, a force to be reckoned with, and I had somewhere to be. That trade show was important. I had to get to Dubai, and no stupid airline was going to stop me. I definitely wasn't going to wait for the Phoenix airport, in its incompetence, to sort out the problem, whatever it was. So, since it was still early in the morning, I picked up my bag, walked over to the rental-car desk, and rented a car to drive back to LA. To me, it was all a big hassle. *But*, I figured, *what the hell?* I'd cruise back home and get on a plane the next day.

About halfway back, my mind drifted back to those damn TVs that wouldn't work. I don't know why I fixated on that, but that, combined with how stinking quiet it had been inside Phoenix Sky Harbor International, gave me this strange feeling in the pit of my stomach, like something was wrong. I drove the rest of the way popping in one CD after another, but that uneasiness churned around in my stomach like a little minion whispering something I couldn't quite hear.

When I finally reached LA at noon, I came face to face with the most frightening and bizarre sight I had ever witnessed. This was Los Angeles, California, mind you—a city of over four million people. But, there was no one in sight, not even on the freeways. Can you imagine LA in the middle of the day with no one on the freeways? Wide-open roads, no gridlock, no cacophony of horns? And, there was nobody walking on the streets. Nobody shopping in the stores. Nobody parked at the gas stations. Everything was totally silent and deserted. It was so incredibly spooky, I felt as though I had just driven onto the set of an old Alfred Hitchcock film. My stomach churned again because this time, I *knew* something was wrong.

Whatever was happening wasn't good. But, the only way to find out was to pray there was something on the radio that would explain the ghostly appearance of LA. Had the zombie apocalypse started? As I reached down to pop the CD out and turn the radio on, my hand shook. I jerked it back once, almost afraid, before turning the dial to my favorite station. Instead of nonstop music, all I heard was news. I turned the dial to another station—news—then another—more news. Finally, I turned up the volume and tried to process what the newscaster was saying. Something about buildings . . . something about fire . . . something about a second plane.

What?

They were talking about damage. I looked all around, but I didn't see any damage in LA: no bombed-out buildings, no torn-up streets, no sirens, no wrecked cars, no screaming people. Just a completely empty city.

Well, there was no way I was going home; there wouldn't be anyone there to tell me anything. So, I drove straight to my office. Even though I wasn't supposed to be in town that day, I knew a lunchtime meeting had been scheduled, and I figured people would be there. Plus, my boss would see my dedication to the job.

When I got to my office building, I sprinted up the stairs instead of waiting for the elevator. When I opened the office door, I was met with total chaos. My colleagues raced from office to office.

"What the hell is wrong with everybody?" I shouted.

They all yelled back at once, each with something else to say. Apparently, they had been busy all morning doing their work and were only now figuring out what was going on, just like me. They hadn't been watching the news any more than I had. One of them rolled a TV into the conference room and turned it on. As we gathered around, things finally became clear.

Two planes had crashed into the Twin Towers of the World Trade Center in New York, and we watched in horror as one of the buildings collapsed. They were replaying footage recorded hours earlier. We had missed the whole thing and were just now getting up to speed. It was hard to fathom, yet there it was on the TV: smoke pouring out of both buildings, people running helter-skelter covered in white ash, office workers jumping to their deaths to escape the fire.

I thought I was going to be sick. That feeling in the pit of my stomach had been trying to tell me all was not well with the world. With growing horror, I realized I had friends who worked in the Twin Towers. I wondered, *They weren't in those buildings when they collapsed, right? And, hold on a minute . . . what about us? Are they going to attack Los Angeles? Who are they?* My head began to spin so rapidly, I had to sit down.

Then, out of the chaos, I heard my boss say something I'll never forget: "Vinny, make sure you call your reps in New York and tell them not to stop working. The Twin Towers are in Lower Manhattan, and they can still work in Midtown."

"What the hell are you talking about?" I said. "There's a mass exodus of people walking across the Brooklyn Bridge. New York, and maybe all of America, is under attack. No one is working."

"Well, Upper Manhattan, Harlem, and Midtown are fine!" my boss shrieked. "I told you to call all your reps to get back to work."

I'd been working with him for several years. Despite his volatile personality, he'd given me my first paying job in the beauty industry. It had been an opportunity to travel the world in style on his dime. And, it paid a boatload of money. Everyone in the office agreed that our boss had always been nuts—tossing over the conference table, yelling, hiring and firing with abandon, harassing female employees—but his lack of sensitivity on that day was the last straw.

There was no way I wanted to continue working for that man. Although I was tempted to pack up my belongings and walk out the door right then and there, I sucked it up and gave him forty-five days' notice so I could keep my already-scheduled out-of-town appointments. Not working was out of the question. I had bills to pay, lots of them. Although my goal had always been to develop my own line of products to help people look and feel beautiful, a part of my yearning had been to improve my own appearance. But, I wasn't ready to fly on my own. I didn't yet have all the skills or the financial backing to turn that dream into reality. So, although the mere thought of working again under someone else's thumb made me physically ill, I resigned myself to finding another salaried job, learning more about developing products, and biding my time.

After a while, I realized that I had learned several things on that fateful morning. First, most of the hijackers were from Saudi Arabia, right next door to Dubai, the very place I was so desperate to go to; and second, a friend from my high school had been killed. I was still in shock over the horrific events in New York that September day, but something else became indelibly imprinted on my psyche. Regardless of where I had to work or for how long, I would never abandon my goal to one day work for myself.

Functional Dysfunction

G rowing up, other boys loved sports and rough-and-tumble stuff. Not me. I preferred playing with dolls with my cool sister, Teri, who is three years older than me. I especially loved it when she wanted to dress up and borrow my mom's makeup. Truly, whatever she wanted to play, I was in. It wasn't because I was gay—I had no idea what that even was at the time—but because I loved her. And, playing with girl toys didn't "turn me gay." That's not the way it works. I simply wanted to hang out with my older sister.

Those were good times with Teri, times to savor. However, it did me no favors with the boys in the neighborhood. Although I wanted to be "normal," other kids always teased me. My nose looked like a beak, I was skinny and awkward, and I had a lisp. So, as much as I wanted to fit in, I didn't have a clue how to do it.

Suffice to say, reality was never as fun for me as what I saw on the '80s TV shows I watched with my Grandmother Serra. For some reason, my mom's mother didn't think voraciously watching *The Young and the Restless* and *Dynasty* would hurt eight-year-old me. I'd stop by her house every day after school, and we'd sit on the couch and watch together. I think, even then, she could see in my eyes a passion for beauty and just how enthralled I was with the glitz, the glamour, the money, and the drama. Both shows laid the foundation for my adult life.

The family in *The Young and the Restless* was the Abbotts. Their business was called Jabot, and they created and sold a fancy line of cosmetics. I was attracted to their lives like a hammer to a nail. It was all so glamorous. I loved the idea of creating a unique fragrance, something no one else had ever created, and putting the fragrance into these incredible little bottles, like works of art unto themselves. If you think about it, the whole fragrance business is amazing. You put this package together, and it's just a tiny amount of liquid in a fancy bottle. Yet, people will pay crazy money for it.

By the time I was ten years old, I knew I wanted to launch a line of beauty products that would far exceed the success of the fictional business Jabot. Other people may think watching soap operas is a stupid waste of time, but I owe *The Young and the Restless* a lot. It's where all my beauty aspirations were born.

Since Jabot was primarily about perfume, the first products I tried to develop went in the same direction. I was probably about ten years old when I first started creating my own perfumes. While other boys my age were padding up for football practice, shooting hoops, or doing whatever it is that so-called "normal" boys do, I would try and recreate the bottle designs I saw on the show. I even started thinking up names for my perfumes. The very first name I came up with was "VS Vincenzo," a combination of my first and last names in Italian, and I knew when I launched my cosmetic line one day, it would be called that.

However, *The Young and the Restless* paled in comparison to the gloriously dramatic trials and tribulations of the fabulously wealthy in *Dynasty*. From the moment I saw Heather Locklear, Emma Samms, Linda Evans, and John Forsythe on the screen, I was hooked. I loved the incessant beauty, the cars, the house, the jewels, and the clothes. I remember sitting on my grandmother's lap, gazing at it all. They had everything I wanted: power, strength, beauty—a dynasty.

Unfortunately, when you merge the power-hungry backstabbing of *Dynasty* with the over-the-top drama of *The Young and the Restless*, you end up with an alternate reality, one I was all too happy to embrace. These shows teleported me into the world of the rich and powerful to a place where I could find the new reality I'd painted for myself. I envisioned a life of wealth, power, and luxury, a life where people served you day and night. The element of power was especially appealing. With that type of money and power, I could buy what I wanted when I wanted it, and it would make me happy. I could even control my business empire and make things the way I wanted them to be.

On a deeper level, another thing that attracted me to *Dynasty* was something I don't think I comprehended until I was much older. The first gay character ever on national television was on *Dynasty*: Steven Carrington. The "gay thing" has always been a sensitive topic in our culture, and the way it was presented on the show was negative. The writers were just reflecting the general attitude of the times, I'm sure. The dialogue was harsh toward Steven, and it was always clear that the other characters strongly believed he had to change.

As for me, I wasn't sure what to think about it. I was too young. But, their severe treatment of Steven definitely confused me and gave me a slightly uneasy feeling. They were perpetuating a stereotype: that being gay was wrong. As a good Catholic boy, I knew being gay was a sin, as it was a topic priests often talked about from the pulpit. But, therein lay my confusion. Even then, I think I knew a person who was truly gay can't just change. They can't just become heterosexual because society thinks they should. It doesn't work that way. It's almost comical to think about it now.

At one point in the show, an oil-rig explosion badly injured the Steven character. I thought they were going to kill him off and was so upset, but they didn't. No, instead of killing the character off, they brought in another actor to play the role . . . a much better-looking actor. The story was written to say that Steven had been in this explosion and had to undergo plastic surgery, and that's why he looked so different. It was pure soap-opera stuff, and I loved every minute of it. You see, something struck me at that moment. I remember thinking to myself, *Wow, people can get plastic surgery and totally change themselves? Maybe I can do that someday.* It was a revelation.

I was too young to understand, but that was the first time changing one's entire appearance had ever been presented to me. Later in life, those thoughts would resurface.

Dynasty finally went off the air in 1989. I was fifteen years old and cried for a week. I felt like I had lost my family. Okay, fine, I'll admit it. It was definitely an obsession. I remember watching the show and, no matter what was going on around me, having total tunnel vision. Then, I would think about it afterward and how I was going to be exactly like them, and a warm peace would surround me. It was as if I knew all would be right with the world—just as soon as I had built my empire, that is.

DIVE THE DEPTHS

You don't have to be from a dysfunctional family to become famous, but it helps. My parents named me Vincenzo Michelangelo Spinnato (after St. Michael). I was born in Philadelphia, Pennsylvania, an hour from Atlantic City. Although my parents raised me with strong values, there was always this hidden backdrop of gambling, debauchery, and greed calling to me from Atlantic City. I think my attraction to it was really more about the posh interiors, posh automobiles, and posh people of some of the high-end casinos in that town. There is so much money floating around, you can almost smell it.

As you may be able to tell from my name, my family is staunchly Italian, and maybe more importantly, staunchly Catholic. When you put those two together, it's like mixing water with powdered mortar; you get cement. I was living inside the walls of a house that was rigid, unbending. Yet, what I needed was a place where I could grow into the person I knew I had to become. My family looked, acted, and felt one way, while I looked, acted, and felt another. As I became older, I realized I had always been completely uncomfortable in my own skin. It was hard to figure out why, but it was probably because I felt different from everybody else on the inside, as well as the outside. It was as if I was this person who had been dropped into a family the total opposite of me.

Creative people like me, freethinkers who have an entrepreneurial bone driving them, forcing them forward, have a hard time growing up under strict constraints. We don't feel able to express ourselves. Don't get me wrong; my parents loved me and were there for me. But, they came from different worlds, and I was going to have to show them mine: a place where I could grow and flourish, a place where I could create things that were my own, a place where it was okay to be the lavish person I knew was inside of me.

That lavishness was perhaps the product of the stars I was born under (coupled, of course, with my love for *Dynasty* and *The Young and the Restless*). Numerologists have a field day with my birthdate. They say I'm a "triple eleven," born at 11:11 a.m. on 11/11/74 (7 + 4 = 11). The triple-eleven thing also makes me a triple Scorpio, which is, apparently, exceedingly rare. While triple Scorpios have gigantic hearts, will give you the shirt off their backs, and are very loyal, there's also something about being a triple Scorpio that makes one very eccentric, driven, and extreme, which is not always good news. We can hold a grudge for thirty or forty years. For instance, I may let someone who screws me get off the hook temporarily, but five years later, I might let them have it. My dad always said that if I played football, I would sack the quarterback, then go after the family. Obviously, these are not necessarily good traits, but it helps explain the extreme highs and lows in my life.

I wondered why I always felt so different from my other family members, and the bizarreness of my birthday is one element of it. I would have thought that when you combined my mom and my dad, you'd end up with a little version of them. But, that's not what happened. I was something totally different. So different, in fact, I'm convinced that when I was born I popped out carrying a miniaturized Louis Vuitton bag.

From their perspective, parenting me must have been difficult. My mom was a gutsy lady who ran her own business, but she was so afraid something dreadful was going to happen to me, she must have lived under a mountain of stress. You see, when my mother was a little girl, she was watched over ferociously by her parents. Both of her older sisters had died tragically young, so her parents were terrified they'd lose her, too. This led to them holding on tight . . . too tight.

Likewise, when I was born, my Grandmother Serra more or less took me over. I was the total focus of her attention. She "ran block" against anything she thought might harm me. And, since her life experience had been so filled with tragedy, she carried this protectiveness to an unhealthy level. She was so afraid that I would contract a terrible disease or have a catastrophic accident that she and my mother encircled me in a protective bubble. No one was allowed to enter, including my father! I don't think he was even allowed to hold me until I was three months old. It seemed like my grandmother thought he was going to drop me off the balcony or feed me to the lions, or something. Whatever it was, it was abnormal to the extreme. I was being smothered with love, and as I grew, I felt like an oyster outgrowing my shell.

Thus, in those first few years of life, I never had a chance to bond with my dad. Although we had opportunities later to try and bond, the damage was done. My grandmother and mother's rigid behavior toward my father severed my connection to him, yet it did something else, too. It made the connection to my grandmother really strong. She and my mom were the only humans who interacted with me physically, so they're the ones I latched on to.

There were so many times when this protective mania would come into play, even when my dad would want to teach me "boy things." For example, one day my dad announced that he and I were going fishing. Sounds like a pretty good father-son thing to do, right? Hell, I thought so. But, as we got ready to leave, my mom came out on the porch crying. "I want to take him shopping today," she said. Eventually, she made my dad feel like shit. The fishing trip with me was canceled. I didn't realize until years later how hurt and left out my dad must have felt in times like this.

Dad's only escape was music, his true love. He played everything by ear. Once my father learned a song, he could play it the rest of his life, be it on piano, bass, or trumpet, his main instrument. He may have made a living as the director of the Vineland Board of Transportation, but in his heart, he was a musician.

Another music man in my life was my grandfather, Enrico Serra. He and Grandma Serra emigrated from Italy, where Grandpa Serra had been a count who, because of his title, could trace his lineage back to the Roman Empire. Unfortunately, he had to give up his title when he became a United States citizen.

He was a genius with stringed instruments. Anything from cello to bass to violin, he could play like it was attached to his body. He studied at a conservatory in Italy and earned his doctorate in music *at the age of sixteen*. In fact, he was so musically talented, I always joked that if a doctor took a blood sample from him, little musical notes would be floating around in the vial.

To demonstrate his talent, his first job in America was writing the music for the Laurel and Hardy silent films, which he also conducted in the movie theaters. His scores brought the music to life. He was also the head of the New Jersey Musicians' Union, so if musicians wanted to play professionally, they had to go to my grandfather and pay their union dues.

Living surrounded by music, I always wondered how I had somehow missed getting that musical gene. However, my love for music inspired me decades later to create a music scholarship in honor of my father and grandfather.

So, although in the music department I was talentless, I tried to be close to my father—as close as I could be, anyway. The problem was that beyond music, my father was a man's man. He was Army football, all things manly—things that were just not me. Dad did everything he possibly could do to connect with me, and though we got along great, the connection, the bond, just wasn't there. If only I had picked up on that musical gene!

Poor Dad just couldn't figure out how to relate to me, so he ended up doing everything through "stuff." He bought me every kind of ball—football, basketball, baseball—and gloves for both of us. If he wanted to take me hunting and fishing, he'd come home with a shotgun and a fishing boat. I understood that he wasn't trying to *buy me*, but trying to connect with me.

Eventually, I realized that I grew up thinking I couldn't get anybody's love without buying stuff for them. It was a gut reaction to the way my father had tried to connect with me, and the way he had tried to repair things with his wife. Whenever something would go horribly wrong between him and my mom, he'd try to fix everything with stuff. If they had an argument, Dad would say something like, "I'm going out to pick up the dry cleaning," but instead of coming back with a couple of starched white button-downs, he'd show up with a $20,000 camper. He'd say he was going to go out for a cigarette, and then come back with a fishing boat. He was trying to buy love.

Now that I look back on it, although Mom was this wonderful woman whom I loved so much, she had her issues, and she and I didn't have the healthiest relationship. I was such the center of her focus that I felt I had slipped into the role of emotional support more in line with a husband. I didn't have the knowledge to understand that at the time, but that's what was going on.

So, I became, unequivocally, the emotional surrogate of my father for my mother.

EYE OF GUILT

Even if my grandmother had allowed others to hold and play with me as a child, our house was still a daunting place to grow up. My mother had statues of saints *all over the house*. She was more than a little obsessed with them. Some of these statues were as much as two feet tall. When I was that little, they were eye-level to me. My sister, Teri, and I were surrounded by statues of deities on all sides. Our house was like a shrine inside a Catholic-Italian enigma.

There were statues in the living room, family room, kitchen, bathrooms, basement, and bedrooms. We even had a statue of Mary herself on the front lawn peeking out of the bushes, as if to watch over us.

You have nowhere to escape. Walk into your room? There's the Blessed Virgin. Playing with Tinkertoys on the floor? There's the Blessed Virgin. Going to sleep at night? There's the Blessed Virgin. Have an unclean thought? Oh. My. God. There's the Blessed Virgin. There was a huge statue of the Virgin Mary in my room, peering down at me from my chest of drawers. Imagine puberty with Mary watching you *all the time*. Talk about a guilt trip. Every time something impure, as defined by the Church, entered my head, I would look over to find Mary staring at me. She knew what I was thinking, and it was disappointing to her. I grew up with a guilt complex.

My mom was devoted to being Catholic, though. There was never any question of that. All of these statues seemed to me like some sort of insurance policy, as if the image of a saint or the mother of

God would protect us from evil simply because of its presence. And, true to my mother's protective-bubble mania, she and her religion always watched over me. I'll give you one example.

When I was in high school—years before 9/11, when everyone was allowed to be on the tarmac—my class went to Europe. Now, picture this: I was on the plane getting situated in my window seat, when I looked through the window and saw my mother running across the tarmac. She was actually running on the friggin' tarmac, coming toward the plane! When she got close enough, she tried to throw holy water on it. God bless her, but that is how insane it all was.

It took months for my classmates to stop teasing me about it.

MOMTREPRENEUR

Mom was quite a woman, though, protective mania and all. Not only was she a good mom, she was also an amazing businesswoman. In fact, Mom owned her own limousine business, and that's where she shined.

The limos, oh, my God. She owned her own *fleet* of limousines—five, to be exact, and they were always parked in the driveway. Our driveway looked like the filming of *The Godfather* when all the heads of the mafia crime families gathered. I got driven to school in a limo most of the time. It was comical. Because of this, I got invited to a lot of proms in my teenage years, not because the girl was so in love with me, but because we could go in a limo!

It was a pretty amazing thing. Mom worked from home while raising me and my sister. Along with the limo business, she was also a wedding planner and had partnerships with other bride-related companies, making it unbelievably easy for a bride to get everything she wanted in one place. She would book the church or synagogue, and set up the priest or rabbi to officiate. That woman knew how a wedding should go, but more importantly, she knew how a wedding *shouldn't* go. She knew all the little details that a bride would have never thought of, and people loved her for it.

She contracted with a floral company and made incredible bouquets. If you stop to think about it, the floral part of her business was brilliant. Consider what it would be like to own a regular floral shop. You have to put in tons of inventory, and all of it goes bad really, really quickly. But, my mom didn't have to inventory a bunch of excess crap. She could order what she needed when she needed it. Hell, there was practically no waste. It was an act of pure business genius. She even had a connection with a wedding-gown company where she would send brides to select that special dress.

She had created a turnkey business in the '70s, way ahead of the times. I didn't realize it then, but seeing how she put everything together, how she took all the hassle out of a wedding by handling every detail—it gave me *the idea*. It planted a seed in my little-kid brain that one day, I'd take that turnkey idea and use it to build a beauty line: a one-stop shop for everything a company or celebrity needed in order to offer their own branded beauty products.

But first, I needed to survive adolescence.

Sister Mary Rotten Crotch

Elementary schools are usually very sweet, where everyone is supportive, parents volunteer constantly, and teachers are all dedicated and thrilled to be surrounded by little munchkins all day long.

My elementary school? Not so much. Catholic school was *not* like that. For starters, I went to school when Catholic schools had just stopped allowing nuns to smack you. Previously, nuns always carried around those damned wooden rulers, and if you acted out or didn't memorize your homework, they'd crack it across the back of your hand. Thankfully, when I entered the first grade, the rules had changed. To tell you the truth, though, I think not being able to smack students anymore pissed some of the nuns and priests off.

Well, let me tell you something. You wouldn't want to piss one of those nuns off. They were mean. Instead of cracking us across the back of the hand with a wooden ruler, they had us lean against the wall while holding up two Bibles, one in each hand. You'd have to put your back to the wall and extend your arms as far as they would go, and just stand there holding the books. This was a position I became quite familiar with. And damn, those Bibles were heavy. It's a wonder I didn't develop broad shoulders from it all.

Another thing—in my school, there were girls and boys ranging in age from kindergarten through eighth grade. So, the age gap was huge. Plus, we all wore uniforms. I'm talking about khaki pants, polished black dress shoes, white button-down shirts, and of course, the prototypical blue blazer with that patch embroidered on it. I hated it. I had some inner desire, some driving force to express myself. I was an individual, but there was no way I could feel special or unique wearing a school uniform like everyone else. It just didn't work for me.

They expected each of us to squeeze into the same neat little box, and that just wasn't me. When the nuns figured that out, they had no idea how to handle it. I needed teachers with a loving approach who would allow more freedom for creativity. The nuns at my school sure as hell weren't giving it to me.

During class, while they droned on in that same monotonous tone they used, my mind would wander as I thought about beauty, glitz, and glamour. I always had trouble concentrating, and the more they droned on, the more my mind wandered. Then, of course, the nuns would be mad I hadn't memorized four hundred pages of the catechism like I was supposed to. Do you know what happens when the nuns get pissed off? Go ahead and grab two Bibles and stand at the back of the room.

So, what was the result of this clash of personalities? The result was me lashing out. Here's a story to illustrate a bit of my rebellion.

In Catholic school, they do a thing called confirmation. Most Christians are familiar with it, but it's basically a ceremony that means you are accepting responsibility for your faith and destiny. Well, I had a big problem with that. I wasn't even sure I wanted to be part of their church, let alone take responsibility for a faith I wasn't yet sure I had.

For the confirmation ceremony, each Catholic kid was to select his or her own "confirmation name" from the Bible. They wanted us to pick someone who inspired us, someone we could look up to and follow, like one of the saints of the Church. After we chose the name, we'd sew it onto this little cloth sash, along with our own names, and sew the whole thing under our cloaks. Then, during the ceremony, the name would become a part of the kid's name and be read out loud.

They want me to pick a name? I thought to myself. *Well, sure, I'll give them a name.* I didn't want to be part of their form-fitting world, so just for fun, I picked the name Lucifer. I certainly didn't confer with them about the name I chose. I just sewed it right to my sash. To tell you the truth, I thought it was hilarious.

Well, when Sister Mary saw it, she nearly had a stroke. When the bishop arrived and she told him, he flipped out. The priest, though, didn't find out until during the confirmation service itself. Instead of him conducting the ceremony on me, he pulled me right off the altar. He wouldn't perform it. Seeing me yanked off the altar in front of the whole congregation badly embarrassed my parents, that's for sure. It also provided a lot of fodder for the rest of the school. I was practically shunned by the whole community.

I never did get to do a public confirmation ceremony. The priest and nuns were too horrified about the name I'd chosen. Much later, I was confirmed privately by a priest. A drive-by confirmation, so to speak.

Unfortunately, that one incident was the least of my problems. It was the incessant teasing that started when I entered elementary school and never stopped that was the real issue. My classmates were relentless, and they teased me about various things from dawn until dusk. I was a tiny little guy, a lot smaller than my male classmates, making me an easy target. That, and my nose was *huge.* You've heard the term "schnoz"? Well, that pretty much described it. It was out of proportion to my skinny little body. They never let up about that. And damn, as a little kid, to endure that level of constant taunting hurt.

My hair didn't help, either. We beauty experts have a technical term for the mop that sat atop my head. It's called "effing big hair." It was massive, to say the least. You remember those big-haired rock bands from the '80s? Ah, yeah, that was me. It looked like I had a shrub growing on my head.

I'm not sure what was worse: the schnoz, the hair, or the fact that I also spoke with a lisp. Yeah, speaking with a lisp really goes over well when you're trying to fit in with the guys. They think that's about the gayest thing they've ever heard.

That's a lot of crap to pile on a kid, don't you think? "But no, Johnny, that's not all," says a game-show host in my mind. "What else do we have for our little Catholic contestant? Hey, I've got an idea. Let's make him dyslexic, too!" Yeah, dyslexia. Shit.

I didn't get diagnosed with dyslexia until I was an adult. In fact, no one back then knew anything about it. However, I vividly remember its impact on my young life. The shame of our Catholic school's spelling bee was one place my dyslexia reared its ugly head. I can so easily recall looking toward the front of the class at all the kids still in the spelling bee, while I had been the first one kicked out because I couldn't spell a word correctly to save my life. Dyslexia crushed me academically. I could barely keep up in my classes because of it. And, since I had no idea I had this disability, I ended up thinking I was dumb.

I have never wanted to reveal my disability to anyone, be it back in Catholic school or even now. Dyslexia is harsh. It makes you look like a dumbass even though you're not. In school, I was labeled as having a learning disability and put in a separate class, but it wasn't held in a real classroom. It was in a hallway behind a big screen that they would pull across. It was like the kids with disabilities were being hidden from the "normal" kids, something akin to being quarantined. I remember looking at the group of us and thinking, *We're schmucks*, because we learned slower than anybody else. I never really understood why I was in that group. I was too little to get it.

Add it all up—the teasing, the lisp, and the dyslexia—and it equals "poor self-image" and the desire to change my appearance. As I got older, it became an obsession to pursue self-beauty through multiple plastic surgeries, just like the character on *Dynasty*.

With all these pent-up feelings of inadequacy, I rebelled. I used to purposely talk out of turn, and I got into a lot of trouble. And Sister Mary? She would get so pissed. Whenever I would talk out of turn, she'd slam her fist on the desk. It made a big booming sound that scared the crap out of all of us. I used to call her "Sister Mary Rotten Crotch." Once I got mad and called her that to her face, but she couldn't understand my words because of the lisp.

So, that was my early school life: a stress-filled inadequacy incubator.

Lindsay's Jewels

From the time I was a child who was teased and tormented at school, I had a misguided belief that if I gave people lavish gifts, they would love me. It may have begun when my father showered me with gifts, but *Dynasty* probably accounted for my obsession with expensive stuff. As an adult, those feelings only deepened, and I tried to buy friendship and romantic love by giving people a boatload of stuff. The paying for it? Well, I charged it to a credit card and decided I'd worry about that later.

I also thought that if I were better looking, wore designer clothes, and drove a fancy car, I could change the way people felt about me. I told myself that they would look at me differently and be jealous of my wealth and status—the ultimate payback for the slights I had received as a kid from my classmates. Ironically, having expensive things did change me, but not in the way I thought. Instead of making me a better person, they only made me poorer.

But, there was also something deeper going on, something way deep down in the recesses of my triple-Scorpio brain. Somewhere I had picked up the notion that things would solve my problems. I equated stuff with happiness. To me, stuff equaled success, which equaled jealousy, which made Vinny important. That meant Vinny was happy.

Of course, on the TV shows, I was obsessed with all the characters because they were ultrawealthy. They had all this stuff, but I didn't pick up on the fact that they weren't happy. I should have seen that. It should have jumped out of the screen and slapped me on the keister, but it didn't. I was too obsessed with the glitz and glamour that I didn't pick up on it.

I'll tell you a funny story, though. This happened very early on, back when I was just a kid. Even back then, everything I did seemed to have something to do with stuff. It wasn't yet about buying stuff to make me feel better; it was more about using stuff to gain the favor of someone else.

It was the third grade, and I was maybe seven or eight years old. There was this cute little girl in my class named Lindsay, and I liked her. I liked everything about her. She was so pretty. She had black hair, and it kind of curled up on the ends. All I wanted to do was grab one of those little curls, pull it down gently, then let it go so I could watch it bounce back up. I even liked how her name was spelled: Lindsay. I know it's surprising that a gay guy liked a girl, but hey, I was a little kid. I had no idea what the word "gay" even meant. I was interested in girls just as much as the next guy. What separated me was the fact that I was willing to give them what they wanted: jewels.

My mother had this pretty wooden box where she kept all of her jewelry, and she had *a lot* of jewelry. One day, I came up with this brilliant idea. *I know, I'll give Lindsay a piece of Mom's jewelry!* So, I snuck into my parents' room and snatched a shiny ring from the giant jewelry box. I mean, Mom's not going to miss it, right? I stashed it in my lunch box when no one was looking and brought it to school the next day.

Lindsay was so excited when I gave it to her. Her face lit up and her eyes went wide. It gave me the best feeling inside. Seeing Lindsay's excitement made me more excited, and when Vinny gets excited, everything goes extreme.

I brought her a piece of jewelry *every single day for thirty days.* My mother's jewelry box began to empty fast. Finally, Lindsay's mother discovered all the rings, necklaces, broaches, and baubles I'd been giving her. She also recognized that this wasn't costume jewelry; this was the real deal. Needless to say, Lindsay's mom called my mom, and all hell broke loose. All the jewelry was returned, and my mom was *pissed*.

All of this is to say that even in the third grade, I felt the need to buy love. I had to buy it, because I knew no other way. As I got older, I began to recognize a few of these traits in my father. He, too, seemed to feel the need to buy love, and I think that's what happened to me. I grew up feeling like I couldn't get love without doing it through stuff.

This wreaked havoc on my adult life and screwed up more than a relationship or two. After a while, it was all just too much. It was overwhelming. My childhood was filled with too much buying, giving, and getting stuff. So, what does that kind of upbringing turn into? I'll tell you what it turns into: a big clusterfuck of thirty years of therapy.

Pounds per Square Inch

Around the time I was seven years old, my grandfather became very ill. His health deteriorated so badly that my parents decided the only thing to do was have my grandparents move in with us. So, Grandma and Grandpa Serra sold their old home and my parents built an addition onto our house. It's a damn good thing they did. There was no way we could have squeezed two more people into our place.

Having my grandparents live with us brought me even closer to them. They were a real part of our lives, and watching them together was comical. They argued every single minute of their lives, but underneath all that, their love for each other was limitless. I remember my grandmother would get angry at my grandfather and say, "Vaaffanculo!" to him ("Fuck off!"). Then, she'd put a warm smile on her face and ask him, "What do you want for dinner, sweetheart?" It was a true romance.

As I neared eleven years old, my grandfather's health deteriorated. One particular day, everything got really bad, and our busy, loud household was struck with utter silence. My mother and father had gone out to run a quick errand. I was sitting at the kitchen table while my grandmother was at the stove doing what she always did: stirring spaghetti sauce. I looked up at her and realized she was just standing there, not moving. Suddenly, she dropped the spoon and fell backward. Well, she didn't so much fall. It was almost as though she leapt backward. It was strange. She landed across the kitchen table and hit it in such a way that she slid completely across and flopped off the other side. She landed on the floor with a big thud.

She had had a heart attack.

I was terrified. Imagine the fear that a kid has in that situation. I was frozen, unable to move for a moment. Then, I got down on the floor with her. I kept repeating, "Are you all right? Please answer me. Can you hear me?" She didn't respond. We had learned CPR at school, and I knew I had to try it. So, I positioned her head just like I'd been taught, then clasped my little hands together and began the chest compressions. I was counting and huffing, begging her to breathe. I was really doing my best.

I heard my grandfather calling from their little apartment in the addition to the house, "What's wrong? Did something happen?"

Grandpa! I thought to myself. *Oh, my God. He's already so ill. He can't see her like this. It will kill him.* "Nothing, Grandpa!" I yelled back. "Go on back to sleep. Everything is fine," I lied.

I stopped CPR long enough to call my parents on the phone,

and they rushed home and called an ambulance. When it arrived, I was still doing compressions. The paramedics took over, connected her to tubes and monitors, and rushed off in the ambulance. My grandfather must have drifted off into a deep, deep sleep, because he didn't even stir when the ambulance arrived making a ton of racket.

On the way to the hospital, I trembled and sobbed. It was the most horrible thing I had seen in my life.

She was barely alive when they got her to the emergency room, and the doctors did everything they could to save her. But, she didn't make it. When my parents told me she had died, I was in a state of shock, but so was everyone. I then overheard a conversation I wish to God I never had.

You know how people don't really notice a kid sometimes? Well, a couple of doctors were talking about my grandmother's cause of death with my parents, and obviously didn't notice me standing near the door. I heard them say, "We did everything we could to save her, but in addition to the heart attack, her rib cage must have been broken during CPR. The ribs punctured her lungs, so she was unable to breathe."

I was horror-stricken. Instead of saving her life, I had inadvertently caused the death of my beloved grandmother. I fled the room.

As far as I know, my parents never knew I had overheard their conversation with the doctors. They never gave me reason to think they blamed me. But, it's a burden I carry to this day. Even now, I look back and wonder what would have happened if I hadn't performed CPR. Would she have been okay? Maybe the paramedics could have revived her without crushing her ribs like I had.

That sad day, we went home in utter silence. As for my

grandfather, he was still sleeping when we got home. He never knew. Only six hours later, he passed away without being told that the love of his life had died. Somehow, as deeply as he loved her, I think he sensed she was gone.

A few months earlier, I had given my grandmother a stuffed bear that I had bought with my allowance. It was special to me, and I wanted her to have it. So, there I was, clutching the bear throughout the funerals of both my grandparents. I walked through it in a daze. I could hear my mom say, "I want the caskets closed so Vinny won't see them." They were trying to protect Teri and me, but especially me, since I was so young.

I pleaded, "Please, let me see my grandma. I want to give her the bear."

I begged so hard my shell-shocked mom finally said, "Okay, we'll put it in for you."

"No!" I cried out. "I want to do it myself. I want them to open the coffin."

Finally, they capitulated. I peered inside the satin-lined casket, frightened of what I might see. To my relief, she looked like she was sleeping peacefully, just the way I had seen her so many times. I gently put the bear into the coffin. "I picked this for you, Grandma. I want you to have it in heaven." In my child's mind, I thought it would provide comfort to her, and I knew for sure that it would comfort me knowing that she had a special gift I had bought just for her. I tried to be as composed as I could. I whispered, "Bye, Grandma."

The shock of losing both of my grandparents was overwhelming. They had been a force in our lives for my entire life, and I loved them dearly. A print of the original picture of my grandfather playing his violin is in my living room to this day.

The funeral ended and we went home. I started pulling my hair out the following week.

"Trich" or Treat

Yeah, pulling your hair out. It's a thing. It's compulsive, it's insidious, and let me tell you something, it royally sucks. It's a condition called trichotillomania, or "trich" for short. People who have it have an irresistible urge to pull out their hair . . . and when I say irresistible, I mean irre-freaking-zistable. They usually pull it from their scalp, but it's common for them to pull eyelashes and eyebrows, as well as hair from other body parts. Trichotillomania is a type of impulse-control problem linked to something called a genetic body-dysmorphic disorder, where people can't stop obsessing over a perceived defect in their appearance and keep trying to fix it. It may have been in my genes, but there is no doubt that mine was triggered by grief and low self-esteem.

People like me know we have a problem. We're conscious that we're pulling our own hair out, but we can't stop ourselves. It's maddening. The more I've thought about it over the years, though, the less surprised about it I am. It's just another extension of my triple-Scorpio extremism and my unrealistic pursuit of physical beauty.

Like I said, for me, this started just after the loss of my grandparents. Watching my grandmother die like that and then thinking I was to blame—it was all too much. I was just a kid. I guess my system just couldn't handle it. My parents didn't know what the hell was going on in the beginning. All they knew was that they had a kid who was pulling out his own hair. No one knew what to do.

The first time I pulled out my hair was the week after my grandmother died. I was sitting in front of the TV watching a movie. When I looked around, I noticed this little pile of hairs next to me. I had no idea how they got there or what to think. But, that was just the tip of the iceberg. The psychological impacts of losing my grandmother sent me into a three-month behavioral rampage.

It was a destructive phase, and not just destructive to my body, but everything I could get my hands on. During those three months, I got abusive, and everyone around me suffered for it. I blamed my parents for not being there when my grandmother died. I had reasoned with myself that if they had been there, I wouldn't have done CPR and broken her ribs; she'd still be alive.

My behavior got so bad that one day, when they were gone, I staged a fake break-in. It was the perfect cover story for what I was about to do: destroy the whole house. I broke windows and tossed everything across the room. Strangely, I focused most of my anger toward my father. I went into the basement and destroyed all of his musical instruments and fishing poles, snapping the latter in half.

But, the instruments were even more fun. I threw paint all over them the color of Pepto-Bismol. The instruments were completely ruined. Regardless of all logic and reason, I harbored real anger toward him.

When my parents came home that day, I was nowhere to be found. Four or five hours later, I strolled into the house like I was totally unaware. When they confronted me about all the damage, I told them I had no idea what they were talking about and that I had been out riding my bike. "Oh no," I said. "Someone must have broken in." That was the brilliant excuse of my eleven-year-old self. Well, that explanation didn't fly for shit. They knew exactly what had happened.

The first thing my dad said to me was, "Why in God's name do you hate me?" He had always shown me love, and in spite of everything I had done to him that day, he hugged me.

The trich escalated. I began pulling out more hair than ever before, so much so that I became almost completely bald. The embarrassment with my friends was epic. I tried to cover it up by wearing hats, but that didn't stop the teasing. My self-esteem sunk to a new low.

Anyone who has this disorder is obsessed with anything to do with hair. One night, my mother, father, sister, and I were at the Don Rickles comedy show in Atlantic City laughing our asses off. During the show, I noticed my mother had a clump of mascara on one of her eyelashes. I couldn't take my eyes off it. The obsession is part of the disorder. She kept looking at me, wondering what I was staring at. I couldn't help it. I reached over with the intention of just touching the lashes, but instead I yanked them out. I don't even think I meant to do it, but she was really pissed off.

Suffering from trich only added to my self-confidence problems. I was already self-conscious about my big nose, my awful hair, and my lisp, to name a few things. Now I had bald spots to explain, and at that age, believe me, it's not easy. It exacerbated my obsession with finding a way to improve my appearance.

Once my parents realized that this hair-pulling thing was actually trichotillomania, they got me the best therapists they could find. Basically, they did everything they knew to help me. The head-shrinkers told me trich is a way of feeling something and punishing yourself at the same time.

There were a lot of attempts made during this time to cure the hair pulling. For example, I was prescribed an experimental drug that was supposed to block the neural pathways that caused the compulsive behavior. What a load of crap. It didn't work for shit. At one point, this physician had me on four hundred milligrams of the stuff. I wasn't able to sleep much, but when I did, I had terrible nightmares. It made me suicidal, and I lashed out at people. Yet, they kept giving me more and more of the drug. That quack almost killed me.

My parents didn't know what to do. To make things worse, I was getting so much attention from my parents that no one noticed my sister. She took a back seat to everything, as it had all become about me. It's definitely one of reasons Teri left home early and became so independent in her life. To this day, she is still sore over it. It's definitely not her fault, but as a result, we're not close. I know it affected her, and I still feel guilty about that.

My Closet Moment

A pivotal moment in any man's life is the moment he tells everyone he's gay. Well, okay, so not every man is gay, but that doesn't mean I can't dream about it.

In high school, I had a girlfriend, so it's not as if I had a clue I was gay at that time. My girlfriend was a great girl named Cara. We dated from freshman to junior year. Yeah, that's a long damn time, during which I had no effing idea I was gay. I suppose I was about sixteen years old when I first noticed being attracted to guys, but I was still dating Cara and didn't know what to think of it. Talk about inner conflict!

On top of wrestling with these conflicting feelings, I had the added joy of what my "friends" at the Catholic school had told me growing up. They'd made it perfectly clear that men being attracted to men was wrong. "It's an abomination against God," they'd said. Wow, what a trainload of shit to dump on a high school kid. At the time, I hadn't yet figured out what I truly believed where God was concerned, anyway. It wasn't until much later in my life that I figured out that my lifestyle simply wasn't a match to what the Catholic Church was teaching. It's as simple as that. Today, I believe in God, but I don't go to a Catholic church, and therefore don't live under the Catholic tenets.

By the time I was eighteen, things had reached a boiling point. My feelings were becoming a little clearer in my mind. I was attracted to guys, and I knew it.

It was on my high school graduation night in 1993 that I finally came out. I got my friends into a circle and just blurted it out. "Guys, I think I'm gay," I said. I was terrified of what they might think, terrified of what they might say, and terrified of what it might mean for my life.

They all looked at me and said, "Duh. Don't you know that?" They had known all along. To them, it wasn't a big deal. Wow, what a relief that was! Hell, they were happy for me.

The only person who struggled with it was Cara. She and I weren't dating anymore, but we were still close friends. As my former girlfriend, I could tell she was embarrassed by it. I don't know, maybe she thought it was her fault or something. But, obviously, she had nothing to do with my being gay.

Anyway, my friends were so happy for me, they threw me a party. A "coming-out" party, as it were. That's how supportive they were. As the summer opened up, I had a good feeling inside. Although being gay wasn't going to be easy, it was who I was. It was what I was made of, and for the first time, I felt comfortable in my own skin now that I knew and accepted the truth.

It wasn't to last. Things changed in the fall of that year when I went to college. To say that the people there didn't support my lifestyle would be an understatement.

COLLEGE: HORROR ON CAMPUS

How in the hell I ever got into my college in the first place, I'll never know. It started in my head, really. I was obsessed with one particular college, a prestigious liberal-arts school in the Northeast. Its prestige is probably what attracted me, but maybe the fact that it was historic, founded in 1773, was a draw as well. I loved the history and architecture. It was very upscale, very classy. The buildings were like castles.

What I didn't know—what I wouldn't learn until it was too late—was how racist the place was. Keep in mind, this all took place a long while ago, and I pray to God the environment there has changed. However, back then, there was no diversity on campus whatsoever. Out of a couple thousand kids, only three African Americans had been admitted in the prior five-year period. I'm talking about an all-white student body, one WASP after another. As it turned out, racism wasn't the only issue. They weren't just antiblack and anti-Semitic; they were antigay as well. Antigay to the extreme.

Before I take you down the road with me, back to a time and place that nearly cost me my life, you need to understand the backstory.

My grades in high school didn't exactly suck, but they weren't great, either. Neither were my SAT scores. So, when I applied to this college, they turned me down without so much as a second thought.

I applied again; and again, a rejection letter. Most kids would have gotten the hint, but me? Hell no. Despite being accepted to other colleges, I was determined to go to *that* school.

This time, I got in my car and drove to the college. It was about a two-and-a-half-hour drive from my home in New Jersey, so along the way, I planned exactly what I was going to say. To my surprise, upon arriving, I was actually able to see the dean of the university himself. After giving him my sales pitch from ten different angles, he relented. He looked me in the eye and said, "Vince, you've worn me down with your persistence and tenacity. In a decision I hope I won't regret, I'm going to accept your application."

I was in!

I thought that would be the last of my direct contact with the dean, but no. On the first day of school, I found a letter from him under my dorm-room door. *Dear Vincent*, he wrote, *I want you to know that you have the lowest SAT scores of anyone ever admitted to this university. But, you've achieved the unachievable: an opportunity to attend this prestigious university. You did it on pure persistence, a trait I admire. But, I have my eye on you. I'm counting on you not to disappoint me.*

Not exactly the words I expected on a "welcome" letter, but that letter became a mantra for my life. The words were burned into my psyche: never give up. If I could achieve the unachievable once, why not again? And again? Hearing his words in my head, I've had the courage to insert myself in places I wanted to be over and over. I've been willing to do anything it takes to achieve my goal. I've worked for free, learned the beauty business from every angle, and picked the brains of the best in the business, all to reach my goal of having my own cosmetic company.

I got more out of his terse letter than in all my classes my freshman year. As it turned out, the academics were way, way over my head, but I sneaked by and didn't let it bother me. Everything was all so new and exciting.

By this time at the ripe old age of nineteen, my ambition for working in the beauty industry had become my fixation, along with my desire to become better looking. I knew I wanted to get a degree, but that was just a precursor to getting into the cosmetic industry. In fact, if I could have gotten a job in the beauty industry right then and there, I would probably have skipped college entirely.

One of the main assets of this college, in my opinion, was that the school was only about a three-hour drive from Manhattan. Since I was so determined to make my dream happen, I began making road trips to New York to interview with the best in beauty. I'd go into Revlon, L'Oréal, Redken, Avon, Lauder, Dior, and Chanel—all the best—and hand them my résumé before trying to speed-talk my way in. I wanted a job, but I was a full-time student. Truth be told, I didn't know how I would even do the job, should they hire me. I had such a passion for the industry, though, and hoped that passion would come through in the interview process. It never did.

Since I wasn't able to score a beauty-industry job, I settled into academic life. I got really involved on campus, even being elected president of my freshman class. Even so, there was a huge number of jerks that didn't like me, all because I was gay. Some of the fraternities held protests because of my sexuality. Yeah, the social environment there was *that* screwed up. Just a few years before I arrived, a fraternity had actually had members convicted of arson after burning down the Jewish frat house. It was an obvious hate crime.

Around this time, I also learned that the college was being investigated by the NAACP for its lack of black students. Yet, with all the racism, there was one African American professor on faculty. I was lucky enough to take one of her classes. She taught international relations and was absolutely brilliant. More than that, though, her actions that year actually marked a turning point in my life.

I would sit in her class and take notes as she lectured, but I couldn't keep up. The pace was just too fast for me. So, I made a decision to try a different approach. I'd stop taking notes. Crazy, right? But, after I stopped taking notes, I realized it was working. I could just sit and listen, and by doing so, I was able to retain about 80 percent more of the class lecture than if I tried writing it down.

However, this brought on a new problem. The professor kept looking at me while she lectured. I think she thought I was not taking her class seriously because I wasn't writing anything down. The tension between us rose. I was retaining more information, but I was still struggling with the class. Her suspicions soon morphed into anger, and it all came to a boiling point one day.

I knew the tension between us was high, so I set up a meeting with her. I wanted to tell her I was really trying, but struggling with the class. The day of the meeting, I went to her office. Instead of her sitting behind an ordinary desk, hers was twenty feet long and six feet deep. No joke. And, do you know what sat on that massive desk? Nothing but a number-two pencil. It was the most intimidating room I had ever been in. I'm talking *crazy* intimidating.

She motioned for me to sit, then slid a paper across the desk at me and told me to read. I picked up the paper and noticed the pages shaking in my hand. It was a paper I had turned in to her the prior day, and I guess she wanted to see how well—or poorly—I could read. After I stumbled over reading the first sentence aloud, she cut me off. "You're dyslexic," she said.

"What?" I replied, dumbfounded. *Dyslexic, what are you talking about?*

But, she knew before I knew. I was dyslexic! Holy shit! No wonder I had had so much trouble in school. We talked for a while, and she pointed me to a place where I could get help. I have been grateful to her ever since. That being said, it's not like my grades improved much after that. Yet, knowing what the problem was helped tremendously.

Freshman year was grueling, but I got by. It was in sophomore year, however, that things took a turn for the worse. I nearly didn't survive, and I'm not talking about academically; I'm talking physically. The "gay thing" had hit a crescendo, and the haters had had enough of me. That fall, as I ran for sophomore class president, it boiled over.

It was October. I had driven to a Halloween party on the other end of campus, parked the car, and was walking toward the dorm room where the party was taking place. It was dark, and I was alone. Out of nowhere, what felt like a small mob came running up on me from behind. Their hatred went unabated as they severely beat me. In the melee, I fell, hit my head, and was knocked unconscious. I came to sometime later to find my clothes torn from my body, every part of me wracked with pain. I was bleeding, and things had been done to me that I don't like to talk about. I could barely move.

There was no one around in the darkness. I lay there dazed, mostly naked, and in agony. I managed to struggle to my feet and hobble to my car. There, I wrapped a blanket around myself and slowly drove to the hospital. At the emergency room, the doctor examining me said something I've never forgotten: "This is what happens in this town if you're gay."

"Really?" I should have said to him. "Why don't you go screw yourself?"

I had to get out of there. I wanted to go home. I stumbled back to my car, drove to Harrisburg International Airport, and bought a plane ticket to Philadelphia. At the airport, I tried to clean myself up, but I still looked like shit. I just had a blanket around me. I mean, I was practically naked boarding the plane. Thankfully, a stewardess took a fancy to me. She helped me clean up and sat with me for the entire flight. The pilot and copilot were amazing, too. They gave me their jackets to keep me warm.

When I got to Philly, I called my parents and told them I got hurt. The terror in their voices came through. When they picked me up, we drove straight to the Hospital of the University of Philadelphia, where I was admitted. I stayed for about ten days.

I never wanted to go back to that campus. My roommate, Doug, was an awesome guy. He boxed up my possessions and took care of mailing them to me. Later, campus security pulled the surveillance footage showing the attack, and you could see there were about four or five attackers. Unfortunately, it was impossible to recognize anyone in the darkness. If this happened today, the FBI would come in and do a hate-crime investigation, but back then, no one gave a shit. Not in that place.

As for the college, I submitted an official report and talked to a few people from the campus's administration on the phone. However, they didn't take what had happened very seriously. To them, it was more like a hazing incident or something. I mean, I almost died, but nothing was ever done about it.

I'm still furious, but you know something? Through the years I've endured unfair treatment out the wazoo, but I've never let it hold me back. Nothing will. I've never doubted that I would achieve my goal, and I sure wasn't going to let hate run my life.

Earth to Rob

It was about three weeks later that I met my first boyfriend, Rob, through the *Philadelphia Enquirer* personal ads (remember, this was way before the internet). It was Thanksgiving week, shortly after I got out of the hospital, and a couple of days before I turned twenty. I didn't know it at the time, but Rob was actually the personification of all my excesses and neuroses. Had I recognized that, I might have stayed away from him.

You've got to understand, I was very, very damaged at that point, both physically and psychologically. The attack had devastated me, and let me tell you, being in that state of mind isn't the best time to meet someone. I wasn't thinking clearly. I desperately wanted to love and be loved. But, I sure picked the wrong guy—a decision that would happen over and over for many years, mostly because I never thought I measured up physically.

Since I was on the mend, I got a job at Macy's. You know, something to tide me over. Of course, I wanted to work in the cosmetic department, but they put me in fine china and crystal. Not bad for a fashionista like me, but not quite my style. Rob, too, wasn't exactly breaking down the career path working as a manager at McDonald's. However, he was a student at Rutgers, which ain't too shabby.

One day, he came into Macy's and surprised me with flowers. I was overwhelmed. It was then he told me something about himself, something personal. "I'm a dancer," he said. "You know, on the side to put myself through school?"

I was so naïve. I thought, *Wow, a dancer! Okay, ballet, jazz, tap?* No. He was an *erotic* dancer. I should have run away screaming, but I was locked on to him like a magnet.

Rob and I actually dated from Thanksgiving until New Year's Eve. It was on that boozy holiday that he broke up with me. I kid you not. It was fifteen effing minutes before midnight, and the guy dumps me. "You have a phenomenal personality," he said, "but you're not good looking enough for me to sleep with."

Yeah. Not. Good. Looking. Enough.

Shit. As if my self-esteem wasn't low enough. It plunged from the toilet into the sewer.

The date of the breakup was significant, too. New Year's Eve is a time for new beginnings and new loves, but no. Here was "Mr. Personality," a name Rob called me, spending another New Year's Eve night alone.

My whirlwind romance with Rob had lasted only a few weeks, but I was addicted. He was one of those guys who was just really, really adorable. I mean, guys were always after him. Every gay guy in the world seemed to want him. In my fragile state, I couldn't get over the breakup. I stayed at my parents' house in New Jersey for about six months just trying to get him back. I'd call him over and over, but was only met with rejection, rejection, rejection. Really, it was my triple-Scorpio thing kicking in again. I wanted him but couldn't get him, and since I couldn't get him, I wanted him more.

Thinking back on those early days with Rob, I'm embarrassed about the way I behaved. But, it also makes me see how incredibly far I've come and how proud I am of the person I am today.

When Rob started dating another guy, it nearly killed me. This other guy was from Key West, Florida, and Rob had always wanted to go down there. So, when Rob said he was breaking up with the Key West guy and needed to do it in person, I jumped at the chance to win my way back into his heart. But in so doing, I began my first foray into the land of uncontrollable spending. I bought us two plane tickets to Key West. I thought, *Why not? I'll just plunk down a credit card and worry about how to pay for it later.*

I paid for everything. I waited at the hotel while Rob went to break up with the guy. When Rob came back, he told me he had ended the relationship. He then said, "I can tell how good you're going to be to me." I was elated, but that was my first mistake. He continued, "I've got a lot of bills coming in, you know? I could use some help with my tuition, too."

It was the beginning of my financial ruin. After Rob understood I was going to help with his bills, he became much more open to being with me. But, he wasn't really *with* me. I had become his meal ticket, and he didn't want to let that end, so he just played the part.

Not long after we got back to New Jersey, things started to deteriorate. Rob began going on dancing calls again, and everything went sideways from there. I responded by flicking down the plastic credit card again. *Flick*, one semester of tuition at Rutgers, please. *Flick*, two tickets to St. Thomas, please. *Flick*, one brand-new black Corvette, please.

By this point, I was $60,000 in debt. Holy hell. And no joke, I had actually bought the guy a brand-new Corvette. He was ecstatic, but that lasted about a week before he dumped me again. Thank God, his mother made him give the car back so I could sell it, but I was a train wreck emotionally.

The whole thing just broke my spirit. I felt incredibly down about my appearance and nuts about Rob. Losing him was so devastating that I went into a downward spiral of depression. It was deep, it was dark, and I didn't want to come back up. I had never suffered from depression like this. It went on and on. It was so bad, I decided I couldn't take it anymore. I'd end it all.

I hate thinking back to that awful time, but I did try to take my own life. I threw myself onto a glass coffee table. When it shattered underneath my weight, I picked up some of the shards and slit my wrists.

I ended up in the hospital. Hell, what am I talking about? It was the psych ward. Thank God, I emerged from the depression, and by the time I was discharged, I was definitely better, but I still didn't know what to do. All I knew was that I sure as hell wasn't happy. I thought, *Just throw a little money on it*. So, I started obsessively buying things for myself in a futile attempt to lift my spirits. And, what would Vinny buy to make himself happy? How about a thousand-dollar umbrella? That's right. Louis Vuitton all the way. I spent $1,000 on a Louis Vuitton umbrella, something you use to keep the rain off of your head. Nice.

I didn't have a job, I wasn't eating, but I had the nicest fucking umbrella on the planet. Then out of the blue, Rob showed back up. *Wait, what?* I thought, but here he was on the phone, telling me he's coming to see me at the apartment I had rented in Ocean City, New Jersey. Somewhere in the back of my mind I knew he was after money, but the thought of seeing him again was so intoxicating that I squelched the thought.

I had about a week's advance notice. So, I got ready by pulling out the credit card again. *Flick*, I purchased a beautiful speedboat, sparkling white with plush leather captain's chairs, soft-lined carpeting on the deck, and the words *Robbie's Joy* printed on the hull.

The first night he got in, I gave him the boat. Later that same night, with the boat sitting on the trailer at the dock down the street, he broke up with me. Again. I lost it. He had not only rejected me; he'd rejected the boat! I couldn't figure out why the hell he had bothered to come see me.

I cried hysterically, but since I couldn't take my anger out on Rob, I decided to take it out on the effing boat. I pushed against the trailer, throwing all of my weight into it until the trailer started rolling down the dock into the water.

I looked to my left, then to my right. No one was around. I smiled and said, "What the frick?" then walked into the water and swam out to the boat. I pulled myself aboard before taking off like a bat out of hell. In my black mood, I didn't even notice the twinkling lights from the casinos in Atlantic City.

I drove the boat around for an hour until I decided I'd had enough. Since I had bought the boat for Rob, the boat itself had now become a source of pain. I let the tension off the throttle until the boat slowed, then killed the engine. The only sound was the soft lapping of the ocean against the hull. I floated a while, just thinking.

What would make me feel better? The boat and Rob are one, so I'll sink this effing boat. The thought alone made me laugh. It would be like taking my anger out on Rob without actually causing anyone harm.

But, how does one sink a boat? I mean, hell, I'm no US Navy man. These things are built to stay afloat, so this wasn't going to be any easy task.

I thought, *I know! I'll strike a hammer into the side to let the water flood in.* But, I didn't have a hammer or anything else on the boat that would do the trick. The challenge became a comical game for me. *Man, I wish I had a power drill,* I thought, but even drilling a hole in the speedboat would have proven difficult. If you think about it, from inside the boat, the deck is really thick. There's no way to drill a hole from the top and have it pierce through the bottom. After all, it's not as if the boat was on the trailer back on dry land. So, since I couldn't drill from the topside, and I had no drill anyway, I discarded the idea. Nevertheless, I was still determined.

Then, it hit me. Every speedboat has an O-ring with a plug on the other end that is inserted into the hull to allow water to drain once the boat is back on the trailer. But, *Robbie's Joy* was in the water, so the only way to pull the plug was from underneath.

Into the water I dove, fishing around with my hand in search of the O-ring under the boat. I couldn't see shit, but finally, my fingers found it. I yanked once, then twice, then a third time. That O-ring was there to stay. I was foiled once again.

Shouting every four-letter word in my very rich vocabulary, I hauled myself back onto the boat and dropped to my knees.

The entire episode, from inception to rejection, had been a clusterfuck.

There was only one thing to do: Head back to shore, hitch the boat back up to the trailer, and figure out how to get rid of it.

Yet, just getting it out of the water and back on the trailer proved to be a struggle. Finally exhausted, I pulled onto the road and sped away.

But where to ditch the speedboat?

Then, I had a eureka moment. There was a spot near the approach to the Thirty-fourth Street Bridge where boaters could pull off the road, and since it was 2:00 a.m., I knew that it would be completely deserted. Nearly passing the turn off, I jerked the steering wheel so sharply that the boat wobbled on the trailer. For the first time since Rob had left me on the dock, I smiled with satisfaction.

My final act was to abandon it.

Without a single regret, I left *Robbie's Joy* there to rot, envisioning hideous barnacles destroying the hull—a perfect metaphor for my failed relationship.

The next morning, I woke up with a splitting headache and a little remorse. Why trash a perfectly good boat? My childhood friend and fisherman buddy would flip out over a speedboat, I realized. I picked up the phone and told him where to find it.

"Are you freakin' serious?" he asked.

"Dead serious," I said. "I'll send you the paperwork."

"Awesome, dude."

Without a backward glance, I got in my car, hit the accelerator, and left Ocean City in my wake.

California
Dreaming

The pain of losing Rob once more only intensified, and I had a particularly bad experience one night. I'd been taking some prescription drugs for a while, which instead of calming me down like they were supposed to do, triggered my triple-Scorpio mania. I got in my car, which was a bad idea to begin with, and I guess I was weaving down the road and got pulled over. The cops thought I was drunk and issued me a ticket.

In retrospect, I was lucky. It was a miracle I didn't kill anybody. The cops weren't too pleased, either. They took me to the police station, impounded my car, and revoked my license for two months. The embarrassing part of it all was that my dad had to come to pick me up at the police station and then bail out my car. I hated that. I was so humiliated, but it was that humiliation that caused me to wake up and smell the disaster that had become my life. I had no money and had ruined my credit. Everything was screwed.

And, you know something? Sometimes you have to change your environment to change your life. To me, New Jersey had become a death trap.

The last straw came while I was playing a little roulette at one of the Atlantic City casinos. A woman kept staring at me, and the attention made me smile. When she introduced herself as being from a modeling agency, I thought she might just be admiring my looks. Maybe I was better looking than I had always believed!

But, nooo.

"You have beautiful hands and feet," she said. "Have you ever considered becoming a hand-and-foot model?"

I was speechless. Instead of being a real model, the only parts of me worth photographing were my friggin' hands and feet! No matter what I did or where I went in New Jersey, I was confronted with my own inner demons: my heartbreak over Rob; the cruel taunting of my schoolmates who pointed to my nose, teased me about my lisp, and laughed at my academic struggles. I was in such a deep rut, I couldn't see a way out.

Then, it hit me. In order for me to move on with my life, I had to get away from that place. It was now or never.

As soon as I got my driver's license back, I said goodbye to my parents. I told them I loved them and that I didn't know where I was going, but that they had done everything right. I told them the way my life had turned out, my out-of-control emotions, my debilitating heartbreak over Rob, my excessive spending—none of it was their fault. I had to leave and leave now. This was just something I had to do on my own.

So, I got in the car and drove west. I had no plan, no destination, nor any idea where I was going. All I knew was, I wasn't stopping in Chicago, Kansas City, or Denver. I drove across the whole damn country until I hit the I-10 freeway in California. The thing dead-ends at the Pacific Ocean. I stopped in Malibu.

Thinking back on it, it was my "*Forrest Gump* moment." You probably know what I'm talking about. It was my time to put the past behind me. Sometimes it's the only way forward.

I slept the first night on the beach. In the morning, I woke up and rubbed the sleep out of my eyes. I felt young. I felt alive. I felt renewed. Just kidding. I didn't feel any of those things. I felt like crap. But, I was in California, the epitome of glitz, glam, Hollywood, and crazy-rich movie stars who had boatloads of money to spend on beauty products. It was time to fire up my dream to have my own cosmetic company. I had a couple of credit cards that still worked, and they would get me started.

I drove straight to Beverly Hills and Rodeo Drive. I mean, where else would I go? I pulled right up to Vidal Sassoon and got my hair cut. I had them dye it blond. I'm talking white-blond. After that, I got settled into a hotel and immediately made a two-part plan. Part one: I would do whatever it was going to take to learn from the best in the beauty business. Part two: oh, hell yes, I'd need a brand-new Beemer to do it in. With this in mind, I made my next strategic move. I called Santa Monica BMW, a car dealership, and said, "I want a convertible waiting for me when I get there." They whole-heartedly agreed with me, and man, I was so pumped. A new car for a fresh start.

Next, I picked up the phone book and dialed the number of a woman named Juliette. Juliette was repeatedly a guest on *The Tonight Show Starring Johnny Carson* and *Late Night with David Letterman*. She was famous for what were called "kitchen cosmetics," a do-it-yourself way to make cosmetics out of ingredients already in your home. She also had a brilliant beauty salon in Beverly Hills, and she manufactured and sold tons of kitchen cosmetics for people who didn't have time to do it themselves. She was a genius.

You see, the only reason I had really wanted to go to college in the first place was to major in cosmetic chemistry. What sucks is that the cosmetic-chemistry major didn't exist in the United States at the time. So, instead of learning this stuff as part of an undergraduate degree, one had to study chemistry, then find work somewhere, probably as an apprentice, that would teach the cosmetic part. So, here was Juliette making and selling beauty products by the shitload. I knew she would be a treasure trove of information. In our phone conversation, I thought I had charmed her into agreeing to see me. I was so happy.

So, before picking up my shiny new Beemer, I drove to Juliette's salon. I mean, this all happened so fast, I still had my U-Haul trailer attached to my car. I walked into the salon and said, "I want to work for you."

She's like, "Well, I'm not hiring. Who the hell are you, anyway?"

I replied, "We spoke on the phone. I know you don't need anybody, but I'll be here tomorrow morning, nine o'clock."

She looked at me like I was a nutjob. "Uh, okay," she said.

I did come the following day. I worked for her for free for a year. I had no money, mind you, but I was bound and determined to learn the cosmetic industry, no matter what it took.

I took another little job on the side that actually paid so I could have enough money to buy groceries. At the time, the TV show *Baywatch* starring David Hasselhoff, Pamela Anderson, and Yasmine Bleeth was a major hit, and I talked my way into a job in the cosmetic department. My first paying job in the industry! I thought I'd be making up faces, but no. Everyone in the show needed to look as if they spent every day in the sun, so they had to be slathered in self-tanner from head to toe. My job—you guessed it—was chief slatherer. Talk about a self-esteem buster. Compared to the actors, I was an ugly duckling, and working on those sleek, perfect Hollywood bodies triggered my body dysmorphia, further deepening my obsession to change my own physical appearance. And, if that wasn't bad enough, I came home every day with effing orange hands from the self-tanning goop.

Other than the *Baywatch* job that paid a pittance, I lived on credit cards. I kept getting more and more of them, robbing Peter to pay Paul. I moved the money around from one card to another. Of course, that eventually caught up with me. I was in horrible debt, and my parents had to bail me out financially. This credit-card cycle went on for many, many years, and let me tell you something: I don't recommend it to anyone.

While I was learning from Juliette, I found out about a cosmetic company that allowed white labeling of their products. In other words, I could buy their creams and potions, put my own brand label on them, and sell the products as my own. I ran out and had VS Vincenzo labels printed, a brand name I retain to this day. Juliette even let me set up a little wall of my products in her store, allowing me to sell to her clients as long as she got a percentage of the profits. It was good for about a year, until sales started drying up. I knew I had to get a job that paid more than the *Baywatch* part-time gig.

The experience with Juliette was invaluable, and I thanked her profusely for the opportunity. I owe her a lot. I had learned how to formulate cosmetics from everyday foods, sell my own private label, and develop a brand.

I was twenty years old and the future was looking bright. Sort of.

That Must Be Some Fucking Cream!

Well, the future was looking bright except for two minor details: one, I was still pining for Rob and trying to get him back; and two, I was dead broke, despite my little *Baywatch* job. I was afraid my credit cards might either self-destruct in my pocket, or maybe the credit-card companies were going to send a hit man to come get me. Not to mention, the BMW dealership was threatening to repo my car.

When the opportunity presented itself, I applied for a job at the David Michaelangelo Salon, just down the street from Juliette's. Thankfully, on Juliette's recommendation, he hired me on the spot. I should have been grateful, but I'll be honest: my attitude as an employee stunk. You see, it was different when I worked for Juliette because she wasn't paying me. She let me do whatever I wanted. But at this salon, I was working for someone else, and I was supposed to play by his rules. And, there it was again: that driving force to express myself that kept bubbling to the surface. That's where the tension started.

From my first day on the job, I had zero tolerance for working for anyone else. I was insubordinate at every turn. In short, I was a real asshole. Being under someone else's thumb rankled my entrepreneurial spirit. I'm surprised I lasted as long as I did. Looking back, I would have fired me in a hot minute.

With money coming in, though, I was able to get an apartment that I really liked. I mean, my next-door neighbor was the rapper LL Cool J. No joke. He lived right next to me. It was an awesome place.

So, I was working in this salon, bringing in new customers, doing facials, and selling the salon's high-end beauty products. All the while, I was trying to run my own thing on the side. I wanted to sell *my* products, not theirs. I would secretly tell customers about my VS Vincenzo line, my first white-labeled line of products. One of these customers was a woman who, in retrospect, was a total nutjob. I don't want to use her real name, so let's call her Claudette. Claudette was rich. I'm talking about filthy, stinking, wrapped-in-daddy's-money rich. I mean, her father owned skyscrapers in downtown LA or something like that.

She came into the salon one day, and I convinced her to buy my skincare line. She bought everything! It was only a couple of days later that she called and said my skin cream was the best. She was so happy at how much her skin had improved and how much she loved it. *Improved?* I thought to myself. *How can it improve? You're, like, thirty years old. Your skin is perfect.* Anyway, she became my first regular customer.

Here is where I made one key mistake. I gave Claudette my home number.

She started calling my apartment all the time. She would order all the cream I had, to the point that I couldn't keep enough in stock. I kept having to place orders with my white-label supplier so they would make more product with my branding on them. When Claudette would run out, she'd call demanding more. She even called one night at eleven p.m. and said, "I really need your skin cream. I'm desperate. Can you give me a facial right now? I'll pay you anything."

I needed the money, so I agreed, all while thinking, *My God, how bad does your skin have to be that you're desperate for a facial at eleven o'clock at night?*

She came over and I took a look. Just for the record, that woman had beautiful skin. I mean, it was radiant. She darn sure didn't need a facial, but she was ravenous to get one. So, I gave her a facial. She didn't leave until two thirty in the morning.

About a week later, I came home late to find thirty messages on my answering machine, all from her. Thirty! The first messages were normal. She said she was out of cream and wanted to get more. But by the last several messages, I guess she thought I was ignoring her, because she was screaming hysterically and cursing into the phone. I mean, I curse all the time, but this was nuts. She was threatening me.

I was so freaked out, I called the cops. Of course, to them, it was funny. I mean, think about it. You are the police and a gay guy with a lisp calls and says a crazy lady is screaming at him over some facial cream. Yeah, they decided to do nothing about it.

I didn't have any cream in stock, so I called her to say the cream was on backorder and would be here soon. Over the next three days, however, her anger escalated. She was screaming over the phone, "Where's my fucking cream? You're deliberately withholding it from me! My skin is a mess!" She was livid.

Several times I looked out my apartment window and saw her red Ferrari sitting outside. I couldn't believe it. This Claudette chick was a full-fledged stalker . . . over moisturizer! But still, the cream hadn't been shipped by my supplier yet. There was nothing I could do.

I told the building security officer about her. I called the cops again and had them come out. This time, they listened to the messages on my answering machine. "Holy shit," they said. Unfortunately, they couldn't arrest her for making angry phone calls. I mean, it wasn't as if she had thrown Molotov cocktails at me or anything.

I got more and more nervous. Every time I came home, I was looking over my shoulder. I had no idea what she might do. Then, the proverbial shit hit the fan.

I was sitting in my living room watching TV when I heard a huge crash. I'm talking brakes squealing, glass shattering, people screaming. I ran to the window and flung open the curtains. Psycho Claudette had crashed her red Ferrari through the security gates and was gunning her engine toward the lobby of the building!

With another huge crashing sound, her car careened into the lobby. Broken glass and metal were strewn all over the place and people were yelling. Thank God, no one was injured. Although I wasn't down there to see it, apparently the security guard was so petrified that he froze. Meanwhile, Claudette jumped out of the car and dashed into the elevator. She was coming!

She made it to my floor and ran down the hall to my door. She began screaming, "I want my fucking cream! I want my fucking cream!" I looked out the peephole and nearly shit myself. She had a gun pointed at the peephole of my door! "I want my fucking cream! Open the door and give me my fucking cream!"

I ducked so quickly I almost hit my head on my own knees, then cowered in my hall closet. Minutes later, with her freaking out just outside my door, I heard sirens as police and fire crews raced to the scene. When they got there, I heard the police come up and drag her away. People were crying and asking each other what happened. I've never been that scared before.

In the aftermath, the LA County prosecutor went after her, and she went to trial. However, with all his wealth, her father easily got her off the hook. Apparently, this had happened a few times before. After that, I started asking around about her and found out that everyone in the Beverly Hills beauty business knew her, and her reputation was not good.

But, that crazy night back at my apartment, just after Claudette was hauled away, LL Cool J came out into the hallway. He had obviously heard everything. He walked slowly over to me, paused, and said, "Dude! That must be SOME fuckin' cream!"

Decapitated

Around this time, as the BMW dealership continued their threats to repo my Beemer, I also suspected my landlord was preparing an eviction notice. Since my finances were in the crapper, I was getting understandably depressed. So, what did I do? In typical Vinny style, I decided I needed some cheering up. It was time to spruce the apartment up a bit!

I rented a bunch of really expensive furniture and purchased artwork to match. One of my favorite artists is Robert Wyland. For me, no one is better, so I purchased three of his paintings and hung them in my apartment. Another artist I really like is Julie Carson, who is a fabulous sculptor. I bought a beautiful mermaid piece from her to hang on the wall. It's basically a life-sized sculpture of a mermaid, just without the head. It's really amazing.

To be honest, I couldn't tell you why I thought this would solve my problems. Maybe it was because I was depressed, or maybe I just wanted to impress people. Whatever the reason, I responded in my usual manner. *Flick* went the credit card, and voila, I had myself the most posh pad in LA.

Since I was about to be bankrupt and with New Year's Eve fast approaching, I figured, *Why not usher in the new year with a gala bash? It's only money.* I decided that this party would be epic. I spared no expense for this black-tie affair, my sayonara moment to all my gorgeous stuff. I invited one hundred people. I had the party catered, serving only the best: Peking duck and fresh lobster. My place was decked out with my favorite possessions on display, and it was a smash. People gathered around the paintings and the sculpture, and all you could hear were *ooh's* and *ah's*. I soaked it up.

The bash cost me $5,000. Ouch.

After that, as you can imagine, things got steadily worse. As if I didn't have enough trouble, the Michaelangelo Salon burned to the ground, and I was once again out of a job. All of my rented fine furniture was repossessed. In the end, the entire apartment was empty, save for my beloved paintings and mermaid sculpture that I had purchased outright. I had no couches, no chairs, no TV. There was no bed—nothing! The only way I could conduct business was to sit on the floor with my phone and fax machine. Although expected, it was awful.

At this point, I was more than two months behind on my rent, and they were ready to toss me out on the street. Thankfully, a friend told me I needed to protect myself legally, so she introduced me to an attorney named Fred. Of course, I had no money to pay him, so I said, "Fred, I'm going to have a multimillion-dollar cosmetic company one day, and the only way you can work with me is if you agree to do it pro bono, at least until I can afford it." You won't believe it, but he agreed! Fred is one of the greatest guys on earth, and he's still my attorney to this day. He helped protect me against my creditors while I got back on my feet.

In my dire money situation, Fred urged me to sell my Wyland paintings and Julie Carson mermaid sculpture to appease the creditors. I finally decided I had no choice. I put out the word, and it wasn't long before I found a buyer. The guy lived way the hell over in Scottsdale, Arizona, so I got into my BMW—taking full advantage before it, too, was repossessed—and put the top down. I loaded the three paintings in the back and took off across the desert.

As I drove through the Arizona flatland (and by "drove," I mean speeding like a bat out of hell), I had the radio blasting. It was an incredible day: sunny and warm, with a cloudless blue sky. I was feeling good. When I finally glanced in my rearview mirror, the blue lights surprised me. Holy crap, blue lights!

I rubbed my eyes, slowed down, and pulled over. There were two cop cars, not just one. Once they came to a stop behind me, the cops jumped out and started yelling at me, "Get out of the car! Get out of the car right now!"

"Why were you going so fast?" one demanded.

Before I could answer, the other added, "You know we clocked you at one hundred and forty-three miles per hour?"

I had no friggin' idea I had been going that fast, but needless to say, they were pissed. They tossed me into the back and hauled me to the station for questioning. They impounded my precious Beemer—ironic, since it was about to be repossessed, anyway—and confiscated my paintings. Why? Because Wyland was so famous that the cops knew how valuable they were. They thought I had stolen them, and I had to prove the paintings were mine. I ended up being fined. Not just for speeding, mind you. No, my charge was a little more serious than that. Since I had been driving at, like, ninety miles per hour over the speed limit, the charge was attempted assault with a deadly weapon, and the *car* was the deadly weapon. Oh, shit.

It turned out to be a $10,000 fine. I lost my driver's license for two and a half years, and I never made it to Scottsdale. Not only that, Arizona revoked my driving privileges in that state for *five years*. At the time, I was licensed to drive in only forty-nine states and Puerto Rico.

But, that wasn't the end of it. Now, I not only had no money, I had less than no money, and this time the creditor was the criminal justice system. Not an entity to which you want to be in debt.

At that point, my friend Amy from Santa Monica BMW came to the rescue. She lent me money to get the Beemer out of car jail, and she eased me through the process of relinquishing my precious car back to the dealership where she worked. Finally, she sat me down and said, "Vinny, you have to get a job. A *paying* job, I mean." Crap, I knew she was right. I had to do it, and fast.

Amy was a true Godsend. She came over one evening and helped me pack everything I owned into my Louis Vuitton luggage, then she let me come stay with her. We grabbed my paintings, the life-size Julie Carson mermaid sculpture, and threw them into the car. I remember being paranoid when we were loading the mermaid sculpture because I was afraid it would get scratched or damaged. To be safe, we wrapped a blanket over it and eased it into the trunk. Before we pulled away, I turned around and bid farewell to my apartment. It was a sad night.

No more than five minutes later, a couple of cop cars rolled up behind us with lights and sirens blaring. We pulled over, and the officers jumped out of their cars with their guns drawn. I was freaked out. "Do they think we're filming a movie here?" I said to Amy. I had no idea what was going on.

One of the cops started talking through his loudspeaker. "Slowly get out of the vehicle with your hands in the air."

"What the *fuck*?" I said, but we complied. I stood outside the car with my hands way the hell up over my head, shaking like a leaf. The cops came up behind us, and one reached into the car and popped the trunk open. Then, he started reaching around in there. What we didn't know was that someone at the apartment had seen us load the mermaid, wrapped in a blanket, into the trunk. Since the mermaid was headless, this person thought we were loading a woman's decapitated body. Holy shit!

When the cops saw what it was, they started laughing. It took me a minute, but I finally started laughing, too.

After the cops left, Amy and I drove to her place, where I ended up staying for about six months. During that time, I felt like a failure. I wondered how I would ever dig myself out of this mess. As for the $10,000 fine I had incurred, I did end up selling the Wyland paintings, and I used that money to help pay the fine off.

And, in the quiet times, I thought about Rob.

Lauren's Linguini

With no salary coming in, money got *a little tight*, you might say. Well, it got more than a little tight. But, listen, this wasn't the worst my finances ever got, believe me. Luckily, I still had connections I had forged while working at Michaelangelo, and there was one connection you won't believe: the actress Lauren Bacall.

I had told her all about my beauty line and given her my business card. She said, "Dahling, we must have lunch. You can tell me all about it." So, here I was, this nobody with a white-labeled line of beauty products. I had no money, my car had been repossessed, and she's this huge movie star wanting to meet me for lunch! What was I going to say? No? Of course not. I was jumping up and down just at the thought of it. "Lauren Bacall actually wants to meet me!" I said.

The lunch was to take place at this fabulous five-star restaurant across town. Finally, the obvious hit me. "My fricking car got repo'd. How am I going to get there? I guess I'll take the bus. Wait a minute, how am I going to pay for lunch?"

The funny thing was, I had never ridden the bus before. I'm talking *never*, not even in New Jersey when I was a kid. Back then, I was chauffeured everywhere in one of the limos my mom owned. Hell, I didn't even know how to ride the bus. But, I put all my moisturizers and products in this elaborate bag and walked to the bus stop to try to figure out what to do. The bus came and I got on. I didn't even know how much it was going to cost. Fortunately, the bus driver took pity on me. He told me I was on the right bus and showed me how to pay. I even had to ask the guy what to do when I wanted to get off. Yeah, I was that bus-clueless.

I would have been mortified if Lauren Bacall had seen me get off that thing. So, I made damn sure I would get to the restaurant well ahead of her. When the bus was about two blocks from the restaurant, I pulled the little cord to make the bell go ringy-dingy and got off. I schlepped my bag over to the restaurant and went inside.

They took me to the table, and I waited for her to arrive. I was so excited, my knees were knocking together. I had never been to this restaurant before, and to distract myself from the nerves, I took in the ambiance. It was a beautiful place with an outdoor patio–feel, right down to the cobblestone floor.

And then, it happened. She walked in. I swear, it was like a scene out of a movie. Oh. My. God. Lauren effing Bacall. I mean, we had met once before, but she was so gorgeous. She had on this beautiful white designer suit, a big hat, and a white fur stole wrapped around her arms. She was the picture of elegance. She walked right to the table, slid ever so elegantly into the chair, and as the waiter breezed up, she looked up at him and said, "Dahling, get me a cigarette," then laughed. She was joking, but they still got her a cigarette. "Dahling, tell me about your product line," she said after taking a drag. "I hear it's just divine!"

I was mesmerized, but at the same time, crazy nervous about having lunch with someone as physically beautiful as Lauren Bacall. To compensate for what I perceived as my lack of good looks, I desperately wanted to appear professional and elegant, too. I pulled out all my beauty products. I'm talking, like, thirty little bottles of this and that, and I placed them on the table. The waiter came by and set down a glass of red wine for her. Then I did something only someone as nervous as I was would do: I placed my designer bag on the table as well.

If you're wondering why that wouldn't be too smart, let me tell you. Remember how I said the place had a cobblestone floor? Well, that meant the table legs were uneven, and it had a little wobble to it. Well, actually, it didn't have a little wobble; it had a lotta wobble. Once I placed the bag on the table, the whole thing tipped and some of her wine sloshed out.

She lunged to grab the glass and I began to apologize profusely. She said, "That's all right, dahling." The waiter rushed over and started cleaning the wine off the table, but I was so freaked out, I jerked the rag out of his hand and began to wipe the mess up. In so doing, I accidentally slapped red wine all over Lauren Bacall. She recoiled.

Now Lauren Bacall had red wine all over her white suit. Everybody began running around trying to clean her up, and finally they got the table set back straight. Now, mind you, we're talking about Lauren Bacall here: the very embodiment of elegance and grace. At this point, she was still very cordial, but to be honest, she was getting a bit perturbed.

They finally brought us our food, and by this time I was such a wreck that as I went to lean my elbow on the table, I accidentally clipped the corner of my plate. The plate flipped up and linguini went everywhere! Some hit me, some hit the floor, most hit the table, but yes, Lauren Bacall got "decorated," too.

After that, she jumped up and said, "That's it. I'm done! I'm going home." She threw a bunch of money on the table and left. I had only shown her a few of my products, but needless to say, I never heard from her again.

My first brush with stardom and I blew the opportunity. In my zeal to appear elegant and in control by looking my best, I totally screwed up. It was another blow to my self-esteem, but hey, at least the red wine was a good pairing to the linguini.

Start Spreading
the News

Although Amy opening her home to me was massively generous, after a while we got on each other's nerves. I knew it wouldn't be long before I would need to get my own place, but my life was a clusterfuck. I was broke, I had no job, I was living in someone else's place, no one was financially backing me to build my own line of beauty products, and Rob was still on my mind. Plus, I felt I was butt ugly. My life was just suck, suck, suck.

Then, out of nowhere, I met an editor at *Vanity Fair* magazine, one of many I had met in my early quests to sell cosmetics. After all, editors love to meet the "up-and-comers" in the beauty industry, because they are likely to become huge advertisers in their magazines in the future.

In my eyes, *Vanity Fair* is THE magazine of popular culture and fashion, which I love, and this lady editor was so awesome. I had been reading magazines like *Vanity Fair*, *Vogue*, *Harper's Bazaar*, and *Elle* since I was a kid. I mean, Mom had them all over the house.

In our one conversation, the *Vanity Fair* editor just blurted out, "Hey, we're going down to Frank Sinatra's birthday party tomorrow night. Do you want to come along?" I mean, it was nuts. But then again, this is *California* we're talking about here. People with connections like this are all over the place.

I was dumbfounded and said the first thing that popped into my head: "Does the pope shit in the woods?" She laughed and told me she'd get my name on the invite list, and that I could even bring someone.

My friend Amy wasn't really into Sinatra, so on the evening of the event, I invited two of my other friends to go with me. I'm not sure if they were more excited to see Sinatra than I was, but I was positively giddy. I was dying to meet Frank and kept daydreaming about who else might be there: other movie stars, famous designers? The three of us got dressed to the nines and jumped in the back of a rented limo, then off we went.

The birthday party was to be held at the Shrine Auditorium in LA. The Shrine is a landmark venue on the National Register of Historic Places, and is absolutely spectacular. My excitement built upon itself. I had grown up with Frank Sinatra's music. Between my grandfather and my father, music like his was always in our house, and Sinatra meant a lot to me. In some ways, his music connected me to the happier parts of my childhood, and I loved him for that.

When we arrived, the ballroom was already filled. It was *the* place to be. There was energy in the air, a vibration. I felt like anything could happen. We knew we had walked into something special. There were celebrities galore! Katharine Hepburn, Tom Cruise, and Johnny Depp caught my eye, but then I saw *him*: Frank Sinatra. There he stood, large as life. As he made conversation with people, he wobbled, then wobbled some more, and a little of his drink spilled. Holy crap, Frank Sinatra was drunk! In fact, he wasn't just drunk; he was hammered.

I was a little disturbed by it at first. I don't know, I guess I never thought of him that way. Then I thought, *Why not? It's the guy's birthday, for God's sake. Let him have his fun.* That, however, was before he was handed a microphone. People started chanting to him, begging him to sing, and everyone just knew the guy was going to do it. Frank Sinatra wasn't just a singer; he was the music itself.

"Start spreading the news!" someone yelled, then another yelled the same thing. I was so excited, I squeezed my friends' hands hard enough that they both smacked me.

The music kicked up in the background and Frank, a sloshing drink in one hand, a mic in the other, started belting it out. This is when my heart sank. He sang, "Start spreading the motherfucking news . . ." My shoulders slumped. He sounded like shit. Even though this was *his* song, and it was *his* birthday, he was trashing a piece of music that you just don't trash. He was trashing a piece of my childhood. I was crushed.

With effort, I pushed my disappointment aside. This was a perfect venue for connecting with the rich and famous who could help me launch my business, after all. I went into full tilt, meeting and schmoozing with anyone and everyone. It paid off big time. I met a wonderful woman named Ellen Sullivan. Ellen worked at *Elle* magazine and had lots of connections. We hit it off immediately. As I did with all the people I met at that time, I told her about my plans to build a beauty line, and she listened with great interest.

It wasn't too many days thereafter that I got a call from Ellen. To be honest, I don't know why she thought of me on this particular occasion; she was just good that way. She wanted to help me connect to important people who might be in positions to actually support me in the beauty industry. It was 1997, and the fact that the great Jimmy Stewart had just passed away, while sad, offered a perfect opportunity to meet the higher-echelons in Beverly Hills. Ellen invited me to the funeral, and while it sounds terrible, I was thrilled.

The funeral took place at the Beverly Hills Presbyterian Church. The church itself is built in the Spanish style and is a fairly modest, reverent place. What the funeral lacked in grandeur, however, it made up for in its star-studded list of attendees, including Katharine Hepburn, Bob Hope, Ann Miller, Kathryn Grayson, Sophia Loren, Carol Burnett, and Mary Tyler Moore. These were all the people I had loved growing up. Everybody was there, and I talked to them all.

In particular, I made a point to speak to Katharine Hepburn. She immediately told me to call her Kate, which I found so endearing. Her shaking problems were really pronounced by this time. Most people thought she had Parkinson's, but it was actually a disorder called essential tremor. Anyway, she was a doll. I told her I had always loved her work, and she was very gracious. To my surprise, she kept asking about me. She was actually interested in *me*, for God's sake.

Then, I went over to meet Bob Hope. I mean, if you're in a room with Bob Hope, you've just got to say hello. I thanked him profusely for what he had done entertaining the troops for more than fifty years. He, too, was very gracious.

I walked out of that church feeling lighter than air, like my feet weren't touching the ground. I'd just been in the presence of celebrity of the highest order. I had been surrounded by greatness. While this opportunity was premised on a sad occasion, I've got to admit, it was really exciting for me. I made connections, pressed palms, and looked for my next big break.

I know what you're wondering: did I talk to anyone about my beauty line? The answer is no. I had no intention of using an occasion as sad as Jimmy Stewart's funeral to pitch anything. However, after leaving, what I did next was admittedly plebian. I left the church, having just met the biggest celebrities the world has ever known, then walked down to the corner and got on a bus to go home. Yeah, riding the bus home from Jimmy Stewart's funeral—a paradox of epic proportions.

As depressing as that was, I refused to let it get me down. I was determined to make my dreams happen. I continued cold-calling high-end boutiques and salons, making more and more connections where I could sell my white-label products. I called on Bergdorf Goodman, Henri Bendel, Sephora, Ulta, Harrods, Nieman Marcus, Barneys, and Nordstrom. I'm talking about all the high-end stores.

Since I was meeting more and more beauty-industry magazine editors, the ad staff at *Condé Nast* magazine invited me to my next big bash: the Oscars! Holy crap, you want to talk about being surrounded by celebrities. This was the year of the movie *Titanic*, which I had seen four times. I love that movie, and if I can tell you a little secret, I'm kind of in love with Leonardo DiCaprio, too.

The movie event of the year, the Academy Awards. I was psyched beyond psyched. Thankfully, this was one event that I didn't need to take the bus to, because they got me a ride in one of *the* limos—you know, one that pulls up to the red carpet with cameras rolling, bright lights in your face, people screaming, and Katie Couric sticking out a microphone. Well, I didn't just ride in some random, empty limo. Oh, hell no. The limo I rode in was full of beauty icons and fashion celebs. It was "the designer limo." I was sitting there cramped into the back with Ralph Lauren, Donna Karan, Anna Wintour, Michael Kors, and Calvin Klein. I was only in my twenties, and this was a huge deal.

Our limo pulled up behind Sean Connery. The one behind us was graced by the one and only Raquel Welch. Donna Karan got out of our limo first, and I managed to slip my business card into her purse. It was a sneaky little thing at the Oscars, but I really wanted to make a connection with her. I, of course, let the other famous people get out before me, so I was the very last person to step from "the designer limo," a dream on wheels.

Unfortunately, stepping out of that limo turned out to be one of the worst two seconds of my life. I put my right foot out first, waited a second, then my left. I heard about three thousand people gasp. They were expecting someone really famous . . . and then they saw me. They gave a collective sigh of disappointment. *Son of a bitch!* I thought. *Maybe if I was better looking, I would get my thirty seconds of fame.*

Thank God, Raquel got out of her limo soon after, so the attention was drawn away from me. I ran down the red carpet to get to my seat. It turned out to be behind a pole, which meant I was leaning left and right during the whole show. "Oh, well," I said. "I'm at the Academy Awards!"

Being invited to the Oscars wasn't to be my only chance to mix and mingle with Hollywood royalty. After the ceremony, an ad exec at *Vanity Fair* invited me to the after party. I had heard that Madonna was going to be there, so I was freaking out. *Madonna!* Madonna had been a childhood idol of mine. She was my god, and there was no one in the world I loved more than her. Along with *Dynasty* and *The Young and the Restless*, Madonna helped shape my life as a child. She's Italian, like me. She's Roman Catholic, like me. And, there's something about her personality that I related to. I think it was her ballsiness. Madonna was a very big part of my young life, and don't tell anyone I said this, but I even used to hide rosary beads under my shirt like she did. Shhh!

So, I had met "Old Hollywood" at Jimmy Stewart's funeral, and I had met the fashion elite riding in the limo to the Oscars. Now, I was about to walk into a party with HER. I was excited beyond excited.

After we arrived, I confirmed that Madonna was inside. I almost lost my mind. I mean, this was a place where if you walked two feet, you'd trip over one celebrity after another, but all I could think about was Madonna. I saw her across the room sitting next to Oprah Winfrey. I made a beeline toward her. When I finally stood in front of my idol, I opened my mouth, but hardly any sound came out. Madonna looked at me, and I managed to stammer, "Ma . . . dahhh nhhh." I got so flustered, I turned and ran.

I blew it! I blew my chance!

Madonna, if you're reading this, please call! Oh, well. So much for my brush with fame.

Lessons Learned

Up the street from my former job at Juliette's salon was Vidal Sassoon, a huge mover and shaker in the beauty industry. Bottles of the Sassoon haircare products lined every shelf at fine stores, and the business was still growing. By chance, I had met Vidal's ex-wife, Beverly, at a party, and we hit it off. She told me that she and Vidal were almost ready to launch a new line of products. I felt that with everything I had learned from Juliette and from working at Michaelangelo's salon, I could help them as they developed and marketed their new products.

Using my usual modus operandi, I walked into the salon and started talking. I was thrilled when they hired me on the spot. Since I didn't have a cosmetology license, I couldn't legally do haircuts, color, or nails. However, I was allowed to do makeup for his customers, a lineup of beautiful stars on whom I could hone my craft.

Though Vidal and Beverly were divorced, they continued to work together. He got the salon in the settlement and she got control of the brand, so my main job became helping Beverly rebrand the Vidal Sassoon product line. I would go into the salons where the products were sold and help with inventory, then report back to her. I was treated really well while working for them.

I got my first taste of the very, very high-end market. I learned more about how products were developed and used. In fact, this learning experience had such an impact on me, it totally cemented my dream to not only sell white-label products created by others, but to start my own company, VS Vincenzo, and create my own product line. Coincidentally, the name has the same initials as Vidal Sassoon's.

I worked with Beverly for six months while I lived with Amy. All the while, I tried to save enough money to get my own apartment.

FUTONS SUCK

After my stint as an independent contractor with Beverly Sassoon ended, I was so desperate to make ends meet that I ended up taking a job selling futons. Yes, that's right. Futons. Those stupid folding-bed things that pull up into a couch. This was the first time I had worked for a place that had absolutely nothing to do with the beauty industry.

The futon job was, for me, as low as I could go, and the most humbling experience of my life. I ended up selling futons on and off for about two years. As it turned out, there was a very high commission on bed sales, and I made pretty good money at it. Even so, I never let my dream fade away, not even for a second. No matter where I was, I always talked about starting my own beauty business. In hindsight, this made it hard to *keep* a job, because when employers learned I wanted to be doing something else, they were never that interested in keeping me around.

I was and always have been a true entrepreneur. It's just not something I can hide. So again, I started buying more of the white-label VS Vincenzo beauty products, and made every attempt to sell them. It wasn't easy. I mean, think about it. There was no social media yet. I was literally selling beauty products door to door . . . or face to face, as it were. Anybody I talked to, even if they were coming in to buy a futon, would hear about my product line. Fortunately, some customers did buy from me, but needless to say, that didn't sit too well with my employers.

One great thing did happen at the futon shop, though. The store manager was a guy named Ron. Even though I was always hawking my wares, he didn't mind. We became friends, and I told him all about my business plans. Ron may have been the store manager, but he didn't want to be at the futon shop, either. He became interested in my dreams. He was the only guy who believed in me. He'd even listen to me talk about my obsession with Rob, who was still back home in New Jersey.

Ron ended up investing in me, lending me about $20,000 of his own money. With this, I could buy more white-label products, although it occurred to me that these products were totally generic; slapping the VS Vincenzo brand on them didn't change that. All I could do was remember that this practice was but a stopgap until I could actually develop products I formulated myself. Eventually, my products would sell either under the VS Vincenzo brand or as private-label cosmetics that I could formulate for stars who love having product lines with *their* names on them.

Since he handled payroll, Ron took out a specific amount from my paycheck each month until the money was repaid. He was truly one of the most generous people I've ever met. He not only turned a blind eye to my selling white-label products from the store; he actually encouraged it. A customer would walk in, and I'd say, "Come buy a futon and some hand cream." If the San Francisco store owners had been on-site, I would have been fired on the spot. Fortunately, they never were. And, since Ron was an investor in my line, he sure didn't care.

While I was selling futons and white-label creams, Ron and I tried to raise more venture capital (VC) to further develop my own formulations and packaging. It wasn't easy to come by, though. Once a true VC investor is at your door, the pressure is on to produce, which was a problem for me, since I didn't have a lab ready to go. Suffice to say, it was tough going.

We always worked hard at it, though. Finally, I saved up enough money from selling futons to move out of Amy's place and into my own. Things were on the upswing, except for Rob, of course. I gave Ron an earful regarding my unrequited love, and one day he told me flat out, "Dammit, Vinny. This is a crazy, unhealthy obsession. You're letting him ruin your life." I knew he was right. I just couldn't get over Rob; it was like an addiction. So, instead of heeding Ron's advice, I compounded the issue. As soon as I found a place in West Hollywood, I called Rob and bought him a plane ticket. He put college on hold and lived with me for a while.

Unfortunately, and in pure Rob fashion, he'd go out partying every night without me. Partying wasn't my scene, and he'd be out all hours of the night. There was lots of drama. Even though we lived together, we never really touched each other. It was maddening. Rob was seeing other guys, and he wasn't hiding it.

Despite my obsession, as time went on, I allowed myself to think about dating other guys, too. Not that that's a bad thing, but I didn't have the best track record for picking out prospective boyfriends. I did end up meeting a really sweet, nice guy named Neil. Out of misguided loyalty to Rob, I felt guilty even thinking about dating Neil seriously—that is, until I found out Rob had gotten into heavy drugs. It was a huge blow. I needed companionship. I needed somebody to be nice to me. And, Neil was in great shape and really good looking, which never hurts. Keep in mind, though, Rob was still living with me, but we weren't "together." Plus, he was flying back and forth to Jersey, doing his own thing, so he didn't really care that I was seeing Neil.

Anyway, Neil fell in love with me and vice versa. We became intimate. I thought things were going pretty well for the next eighteen months. *Eighteen months.* I want you to keep that length of time in mind. It was after eighteen months of being intimate that he told me he was HIV positive.

Yeah, HIV. He had been HIV positive the whole time. He knew it, and he never told me. Of course, when I confronted him, he said he had planned to tell me in the very beginning, but he hadn't known how much time he had left. I mean, this was before HIV and AIDS were fully understood. It wasn't like today, where it's no longer considered a death sentence. People were dying from it. He was afraid to tell me, and then, as time went on, he fell more in love with me. He knew if he told me, he'd lose me.

I felt horribly betrayed. I was not only devastated, but worried.

Scared stiff, in fact. This was life-and-death stuff. It was a betrayal of the highest order, way beyond anything I'd ever experienced. I could never trust Neil again. It might have been different had he leveled with me from the beginning. We could have played it safe, gotten tested. But, how could I ever trust him again if he had lied about something so life threatening? I had no choice. I had to leave him.

Obviously, I was worried about my health, so I went to the clinic. Back then, it took almost twenty days to get the test results, and I had to repeat the tests every three weeks for six months. I was under a mountain of worry. I kept thinking, *Am I going to end up with AIDS? There's no cure for it.* During that whole period of time, I didn't know if I was sick or not. I was a wreck.

That's when the trichotillomania came back. I began pulling out my hair like crazy, enough to make me look like I was balding. It was really unattractive, which again took a toll on my self-esteem.

Thank God, all the HIV tests came back negative. Thinking back on it, it's a miracle that I wasn't infected. I can't even imagine that level of deception happening today. These days, it's against the law for someone to fail to disclose a disease like that. In fact, if you fail to disclose it, you can be charged with a felony.

So goes another day in the life of Vince.

Pool of Dreams

Even while Neil and I were still a thing, my Rob obsession was not dead. Rob ended up moving back to Jersey, but I continued putting him through school. Looking back, I'm appalled at my inability to cut all ties, but at the time, I couldn't help myself. This meant I was living on very little money myself. In fact, since I still didn't have a car, my friend and manager, Ron, was giving me rides to and from the futon shop every day.

It's a good thing my rent was cheap. That West Hollywood apartment I landed after moving out of Amy's place was unreal. It cost about eight hundred dollars a month, had four walls and a hot plate, and sat right in the heart of gay town. Man, I was living!

This was my first experience being around a bunch of gay

people, and it was so liberating. Everybody in the area had a keycode to get into the gates, and the boys came in droves. There was this great pool right in the center of the complex, and it was always full of dreamy-looking men. I had never been in any place like it, and I was thrilled to be there. Right away, I began befriending people in the building.

Moving into my own place gave me a much-needed kick in the ass, a boost to start working on my business harder. The harder I worked at it, the less interested I became in the futon shop. Considering I wasn't interested in futons in the first place, that wasn't much of a stretch. I didn't want to sell futons. I didn't want to deliver futons. And I can damn sure tell you, I didn't want to put the things together anymore!

After over two years of futon hell, I gave Ron my notice. He was sad, but understood. He had been so supportive, and while I don't regret leaving the futon place, I also don't regret working there. It gave me much-needed income, kicked my butt into gear to get my business going, and provided me a friend in Ron. Really, the one thing I do regret is losing touch with him. When one of his sisters got sick, he moved back home, and sadly, I never saw him again. Ron, I'm not sure where you are. Call me, man!

For my next job, I landed at a high-end beauty retail chain that sold hundreds of brands of cosmetics. The best part was that it had its own private label and created cosmetic lines that other companies sold under their names. This was something I desperately wanted to emulate. They hired me to be a salesperson at first, but I made it clear right away that I wanted more. I told them I wanted to manage a store and become a district manager. Well, my sales were so good that in a span of eighteen months, they promoted me to district manager. I oversaw three stores. Oh, my God, I was earning three times as much as I did selling those damn folding-couch-bed things.

The promotion allowed me to cobble together enough money to buy something I'd wanted for years: a little 1974 Mercedes convertible. This one was pea-soup green, and I called it Linda Blair after her role in *The Exorcist*. After about a year of making more and more money, I had moved four times within the same building, each time into a bigger place.

Having money wasn't fun without someone in my life, so—you guessed it—I called Rob. The fact that he was doing drugs was killing me, but I was still paying for his college. He agreed to come visit me again, and I was really excited . . . so excited that the day before he came over, I went to Rodeo Drive and bought a bunch of designer stuff. Once again, my old patterns resurfaced, and I was trying to impress him in a grandiose way. It was all very unhealthy. When he arrived, four or five beautiful shopping bags awaited him. He was overjoyed to open them, but what good it did me I couldn't tell you, because he took me to rejection city not long after.

In the end, all the money I was making couldn't overcome the fact that my role as district manager had become too much for me, especially the paperwork part. My dyslexia was a real problem, as was my talking to customers about my own product line. The bosses got kind of pissed. I only lasted a few months as district manager before they fired me.

Before I made my next big move, though, I made sure I had a colleague who would give me a good referral. It's a good thing I did, because the next foray into the beauty business was a doozy.

Corn Chowder Face Cream

The next chapter of my life in the pursuit of beauty was a wild ride. I landed a job at a natural cosmetic company we'll simply call "Natural Cosmetics." They were a true, full-line beauty company, and it was certainly a leap up the success ladder for me. During the interview, I met a woman named Cassandra, who took a liking to me and recognized that I had just the right amount of beauty experience: not too little, and not so much that she wouldn't be able to mold me. In true Vinny fashion, I basically talked my way into the place. I was hired as *the* California sales rep. Over time, I ended up taking over the whole West Coast.

In my job with Natural Cosmetics, I would go from store to store and meet with the brokers' reps for that region. I sold them a ton of stuff. This gave me a great view of what beauty buyers were looking for and what inventory levels they were interested in. I hate to be cocky, but people really loved me out in the field. I increased sales almost immediately. I was learning the Natural Cosmetics brand inside and out while traveling all over the western states, not just meeting with buyers, but educating the people who worked in the stores. It was a blast. I'd host these little seminars on the brand, and people loved it. In the process, I also critiqued parts of the brand to the corporate office. I even convinced the owner that he needed to change the packaging.

With so much success coming so quickly, they threw Hawaii and Alaska into my territory. In a matter of eight months, I was promoted to North American sales manager, which included Mexico and Canada. That's when the fun really started! I was traveling everywhere and making tons of money. First of all, I killed it in sales, so my commissions were sky-high. Also, when I was on the road, Natural Cosmetics paid for everything; I didn't have to spend any of my own money. So, all of my salary could go straight to the bank. It was almost like making a double salary. On top of that, I wasn't staying in fleabag hotels during my travels. Oh, hell no. I stayed at one fabulous resort after the next.

However, once again, my dyslexia really kicked my ass on the job. It gave me fits. Trying to keep the paperwork straight was a nightmare. Honestly, there was one major reason I didn't get my rear end fired: Cassandra, the woman who hired me, knew I was raking in a ton of money for the brand. She covered for my dyslexia at every turn. She'd help me with sales numbers, spreadsheets, order forms, and crap like that. I'd give her the information, and she would fill in the sales reports. She was a life saver.

I think back about how much she did for me. She didn't have

to do all that. She just liked me and was that kind of person. I owe Cassandra a lot.

Business really started heating up for me. I started dealing with global transactions and different types of packaging. Then there was the regulatory stuff, like customs and tariffs for different countries. Dear God, that stuff can be boring, but this international experience was unbelievably valuable. It was like getting a crash course in "How Vinny Will Build His Own Company and Make a Crap-Ton of Money."

At this point, Whole Foods and Trader Joe's were opening a ton of stores, and they started approaching me, saying, "We want to do private label, and we want you to be our guy." I've mentioned white labeling before, but there are subtle, important differences between private labeling and white labeling. With the latter, a generic product is created for multiple retailers. Each retailer is able to rebrand the product as their own, but they're all selling the exact same product with no modifications. Without anything to differentiate between them, it's hard to convince customers to buy your brand and not the other guys'. Private labeling is different. The product is created for exclusive sale by a single retailer, and the retailer gets to make modifications. They end up with a unique product that no one else can sell.

Anyway, the Whole Foods and Trader Joe's private labels were a really big deal. I mean, 70 percent of Natural Cosmetics' profit came from private label, and that's exactly what I wanted to do with my own business one day. I learned more working there than I ever could have in a college chemistry course. I also learned about packaging, a vital element in the beauty business. Since every industry repackages their products for other companies that put their own store labels on them, I could give stores my input on the designs. I scored dozens of these private-label accounts for Natural Cosmetics with Colgate, Mac, Estée Lauder, and Banana Republic. These were all my doing, and I was making a killing.

Then, it got even more interesting. See, what would happen is that I would first score a really big account, then I'd sit down with them and figure out what they wanted their product line to be. Next, I would relay that info back to our chemist, who would "bench it," which means actually creating the formulas. I figured, *Why let the chemist have all the fun?* I began to shadow him to learn how to mix the formulations myself.

Man, I loved it! What interested me most was the process of starting from scratch. I mean, actually starting from nothing and creating an entire line of real beauty products was fascinating to me. Most of the stores that wanted their own private label had limited knowledge of what they really wanted to do. So, I had a lot of creative freedom to sell them products I thought would work for them. I learned that, for me, the hardest part of my job was putting the numbers together, which is where Cassandra came to my rescue. Everything else about the job was great. Except, that is, where the boss was concerned.

The owner of the company, whom we'll call "Chuck," was a nutjob. I mean, I've never worked around anyone who could fly off the handle like him. His anger was legendary. He was the guy who would go on to demand his New York representatives keep working on the day the Twin Towers collapsed, the same day I would decide to quit. But, back to my story.

I mean, some of the things Chuck did, if I told you, you wouldn't believe. He was incredibly volatile. He would get mad about something, then flip over a conference table. Later, he might hire several people, then fire them. Luckily, Cassandra really protected me from Chuck. He had fired and rehired her so many times, I think she got to the point where she didn't give a shit about his yelling. She protected all of us.

This guy treated women far worse than men. He spoke in a very demeaning way to the ladies in the office. It was like watching a movie from the 1950s. If we were in a room with twenty men and three women, he'd tell the women—who were executives, by the way—to go fetch coffee or pick up his dry cleaning. It was disgusting. Since I was gay, that left me somewhere in between, so he still bullied me around. The funny thing is, the whole time I naïvely thought, *Well, this must be the way owners treat employees in the cosmetic industry.* After all, I was still in my twenties and this was my first corporate job. I didn't know any better.

Despite everything, I was finally starting to build a name for myself in the beauty industry. This led to me landing more accounts with top corporations like Clinique, KamaSutre, Ole Hendriksen, and retailers like Gelson's, Bristol Farms, and Williams-Sonoma, to name a few.

The money rolled in, but Chuck was never satisfied. Nothing was ever enough for this guy. After enduring his abuse for so long, my colleagues and I finally all got together and talked about it. After a while, I joked, "You know what? Maybe someone should put Benadryl in his coffee. That would mellow him out a little." I only said it to get a laugh. To my surprise, no one laughed.

It wasn't long thereafter that Chuck seemed to mellow. Come to find out, one of his assistants *had* actually put Benadryl in his coffee. Apparently, a small dose calmed him down, but one day, her hand slipped and she gave him too much. He passed out. I mean, he literally did a face-plant into his bowl of corn chowder. It was awesome!

But, it's my out-of-office adventures that are even harder to believe.

There's No Place Like Home

Before I tell you my next story, there are two more things you should know about me. One, I'm a history buff with a passion for World War II, and two, I'm a frustrated meteorologist. Not a real meteorologist, mind you, but someone enamored with watching the weather on TV, nonetheless. For some reason, I love bad weather! I think it's due to my happy memories of being a kid and sitting on the front porch with my father, watching thunderstorms roll in. It was one of the few activities we shared.

My fascination started one day when I was seven years old. In those days, my mother used to tell me, "Thunder is the sound made when angels go bowling." Hmmm, yeah, that's pretty creative.

Well, my dad got fed up and finally said, "Screw that. I'm going to tell him the truth." He took me out onto the porch and pointed at a big storm forming in the distance. He explained to me what thunder is and how it is formed. Around this time, I got totally absorbed into watching certain weather stations on TV. You might even say that I missed my calling. I should have been a meteorologist! I can just picture it. I'd be the only meteorologist on the air wearing the latest fashion trends. People would tune in not only for the weather report, but to see what they should wear that day!

But, all of that takes me away from my story. I had my own "Dorothy" moment one day, and I only wished I had had her sparkly, magic red slippers to whisk me away. I was still working for Natural Cosmetics, and one of my distributors was in a tiny little town in Iowa.

On this particular business trip, I was driving down this never-ending, straight-ass road to meet up with a distributor for a five o'clock dinner. I really had to pee, but there wasn't a single gas station in sight. After about an hour of driving and looking for a proper place to pull over, I was afraid I'd have to just run out into a cornfield somewhere. But, I couldn't! I was wearing a pair of six-hundred-dollar Louis Vuitton shoes. *They'll get ruined!* I thought.

I finally came upon a building and pulled over. *Thank God*, I thought. *Disaster averted.* My Louis Vuittons would live to see another day. That's when things started to get really interesting.

I got back in the rental car and proceeded down "corn road." After a few minutes, I picked up my cell phone and called the distributor, Charlene, to let her know that I might be late, but I was on my way. As she and I chatted, I couldn't help but notice how beautiful the sky was in front of me. I mean, drop-dead, Donna Karan–designer gorgeous.

Which made it all the more bizarre when all of a sudden, I heard this sound: a strange roaring. I told my distributor to hold on a minute so I could put the phone down and listen. The roaring was similar to the sound Niagara Falls would make if a freight train was running through it. Baffled, I looked left, then right, but I saw nothing. Weirdly, this sound was getting steadily louder, and my heart began to pound. I took one glance into the rearview mirror and screamed, "Oh, fuck! A tornado!"

No joke. There was a funnel cloud coming right behind me.

I slammed my foot on the gas and grabbed the phone. "Charlene! There's a tornado following me!"

"What? You're kidding, right?" she said, almost laughing.

"No! I'm not kidding. I'm about to die!"

"Are you sure it's a tornado?"

But, there it was: a perfect, textbook tornado. There was no doubt about it. This thing was roaring like nothing I'd ever heard before and tearing up everything in its wake. I could see debris in the distance behind me being thrown into the air. It was headed right up my backside. I was so scared, I almost soiled my Versace pants.

As I watched in the rearview mirror, it seemed to me that it had changed direction and was now headed away from me. So, I slowed down and turned on the radio to hear the weather report. If you're asking why I would slow down, well, it's like I said—I'm fascinated with the weather. I was dying to get a better look. Being the genius that I am, I turned the car around and started driving toward it. Yes, driving *toward* the tornado.

What a nimrod.

On the radio, a meteorologist delivered the play-by-play. He was speaking so fast, he sounded like he was calling a hockey match. As my car crested a low rise in the road, I could see the funnel in all its glory. I pulled over, grabbed my camera, then jumped out. Keep in mind that all this time, I'm still on the phone with Charlene. She says, "Are you sure you should be *facing* it?" She had a point.

I could hear the meteorologist say that the twister was an F5. As a weather geek, I knew exactly what that meant. Holy crap, the most powerful of all tornadoes!

If you grew up with tornadoes, you know, like me, that in the event of a tornado, one should go to the lowest place in the house, like a basement. If you don't have a basement, they tell you to get to the center-most room, preferably a bathroom with no windows so you can lie down in the bathtub. But, let me clarify: This was an F5 tornado, *and there wasn't a single structure nearby.* There was no bathtub. There was no house. Hell, there wasn't even any pavement left on the street. It was gone, all of it. And, here I was, staring into one of these things. I think my hands were shaking, but I raised my camera and snapped a few shots anyway.

As I gazed upon this monster, the son of a bitch stopped. I mean, it was still a full-fledged F5, and debris—corn, trees, cows—flew in the air at its base. However, its forward motion had stopped. Then, it did something I hadn't planned on. It completely changed direction again. You guessed it: it was headed directly toward me.

"Oh, shit!" I screamed into the phone. "It's coming right at me!"

I jumped into my car and started driving like a madman. Meanwhile, sweet Charlene freaked out on the other end of the phone. As I drove, I spotted a bunch of cars that had pulled under a highway overpass. I told Charlene goodbye and floored it over there.

The roaring noise grew louder and louder. It sounded as though I was now standing *under* Niagara Falls. I stopped the car next to the bridge and jumped out. A woman began yelling to me, "Get under here and let me anchor you with these snow chains!" I ran up under the bridge, and she used the chains like a rope to tie me to a metal support.

This thing was coming right for us. I peeked my head under the underpass to take a look at it, and watched in horror as my rental car got sucked up into the air. It was gone! Just as quickly, it came crashing back down on the opposite side of the overpass as though it had been dropped by a passing airplane. I started yelling, "My Louis! My Louis!"

The woman screamed hysterically at me, "Is there a kid in there?"

"No, it's my Louis Vuitton luggage! It's in the trunk!" My rental car was demolished, and my luggage and clothes were spread out all over the place.

The storm had ripped across the top of us, and most of the bridge was demolished. Needless to say, we were all happy to be alive. We brushed ourselves off and got out from underneath what was left of the overpass. None of us had functioning cars at that point, so we waited around a bit. After a while, everyone's cell signals returned.

I first called my distributor, Charlene, to let her know I was okay, but would obviously be late. She was relieved. Then, I called the car-rental place. The guy answered the phone, and I told him what happened. "Sorry," I said, "my rental car got sucked up by a tornado."

He laughed, then said, "Hey, no worries. Happens all the time."

"Really?"

"Sure, we'll take care of it. We have a location not too far from where you are now. We'll send someone out with another rental car shortly."

True to his word, another rental car showed up not long thereafter. I drove off and made my way to this five-star resort where I was staying. After I arrived, I went into the lobby to check in, and I must have looked like shit, because everyone stared at me. They had good reason. After all, my luggage was all broken to hell, clothes were hanging out every which way, and I was carrying it as though it were made of cardboard. Then, I saw this huge mirror on the wall and caught my reflection in it. Wow, I did look like shit! I mean, I actually had corn in my hair, which was standing straight up.

I looked at the check-in guy. "I'll tell you what happened, but you're not going to believe it," I said. "I've just been in a tornado."

He laughed. "Oh, that's okay. We're used to it."

First the rental-car guy, now the hotel clerk. Man, corn country is rough. But, between you and me? I'm still pissed about my Louis Vuitton luggage.

"Don't They Ever Clean the Floors?"

Not long thereafter, 9/11 occurred. That was the same day when Chuck, my boss at Natural Cosmetics, demanded that everyone in Manhattan keep working while the Twin Towers collapsed and thousands died. I had had enough and put in my forty-five days' notice that I intended to leave the company. I just couldn't take any more of his crap.

However, I couldn't just stop work on a moment's notice. I didn't want to leave my customers hanging like that, not to mention I was still owed a ton of commissions. Thus, I had a prescheduled trip to Canada that I was preparing for. Following 9/11, flights were grounded for a couple of weeks, but I was booked on a flight to Toronto on the first day the airlines were cleared to fly again.

That morning, as I got ready to go to Los Angeles International Airport, every TV station was broadcasting a news conference from the White House with then Secretary of Defense Donald Rumsfeld. Now, to be honest, I wasn't paying much attention. Instead, I was filling my luggage (two *new* Louis Vuitton bags) with many items from my "beautimous" designer wardrobe. I guess I was half-listening to the news, but I certainly didn't absorb anything Rumsfeld was babbling about. I turned off the TV and headed out the door. All I knew was that the airline "rules of engagement," whatever they were, were now in effect.

If I had been paying attention, I probably would have canceled my trip.

When I got to LAX, I was informed that I had been upgraded to first class, courtesy of the airline. I was thrilled and didn't question a thing. I boarded the plane, something I'd done a thousand times, and settled into my seat.

We take off. No big deal.

At this point, I turned to my right. Seated beside me was Eric Braeden, one of the stars of *The Young and the Restless*. You might think I freaked out upon seeing one of the stars I grew up idolizing, but I'm proud to say I kept my cool. I leaned over and introduced myself. I told him I was a big fan and had been following the show since I was a kid. We laughed and chatted for a minute, and all was well.

That is, until some guy seated near the back suddenly jumped up, screamed about killing Americans, ripped open the bathroom door, and locked himself inside. Eric and I stood and leaned over so we could see what the hell was going on, but the flight attendant in first class told us to sit down. After all, we had just departed and were still climbing. The captain hadn't even turned off the seat-belt sign yet.

The flight attendants in the back knocked on the lavatory door to see what was the matter. People throughout the cabin talked in hushed tones. It was freaky, given that we were flying out on the first day airplanes had been allowed back in the air since the terrorist attacks of 9/11. "Maybe the guy just had to go really bad," I said to Eric Braeden. He laughed, but both of us were nervous. Only about a minute went by before smoke started streaming out from underneath the lavatory door. My eyes must have nearly bugged out of my head.

A female flight attendant began pounding on the lavatory door and screaming at the man to come out. With the smoke pouring out, she knew he wasn't just going to the bathroom or sneaking a cigarette. This was much worse. She yanked at the door handle, but it wouldn't budge. She turned to another flight attendant standing behind her and said something. Then, she broke into a full sprint toward the front of the plane, apparently to go warn the captain. When she blew past us, I saw sheer terror in her eyes. I mean, this was a woman scared out of her mind, but I've got to give her credit. She was going to do her job, no matter what. Fear pulsed through my veins unlike any other time in my life.

As smoke continued to billow from underneath the lavatory door, the captain came across the PA system with an announcement. Here I was, starting to come unglued, and yet the captain's voice was as calm as one making a toast at a party. *"Mesdames et messieurs,"* he said, *"en raison de circonstances imprévues, nous détournons le vol vers Los Angeles."*

"What?" I said.

Eric Braeden looked at me. "Crap, it's French. All I heard was 'Los Angeles.'"

The captain spoke in French because it was a Canadian flight, but all over the plane, the Americans asked, "What the fuck is he saying?"

Luckily, someone just across from us leaned over and clarified, "He said we'd be heading back to LA."

"Is that *all* he said?" I blurted.

"Something about unforeseen circumstances, and that we had to head back."

With a gut-wrenching jerk, the plane took a God-forsaken dive as the pilot banked a hard left. I gripped my seat's armrests so hard, I think I buried my fingernails into the leather. My eyes locked on the window as the plane banked harder and lost altitude. Since we had just departed from LA, we could see the buildings getting closer and closer.

"Oh, my God, we're dying!" I said. Everything was happening so fast. The massive First Interstate Bank World Center building was on our left, and we were headed right for it. We all began to yell, "Pull up! Pull up!" At the last minute, the pilot pulled up and the plane cleared the building. I didn't know what the hell was going on, but one thing was for sure: anyone looking out a window of that building had just seen an airliner scream by.

Although my insides had turned into a veritable bowl of Jell-O, Eric's had not. As the plane leveled, he jumped out of his seat and bolted toward the back of the plane. While I pulled out my phone and watched my shaky fingers dial my mother's number, he began kicking the shit out of the lavatory door.

I screamed into the phone, "Mom! A terrorist is on our plane, and he's trying to blow it up!"

She, of course, began screaming hysterically. I told her I loved her and hung up. Meanwhile, Eric was still kicking the door, and the flight attendants were now pushing snack carts up the aisles. I blurted out, "Snacks? What the hell are you doing?" Actually, they were repositioning them in order to form a barricade to block off the cockpit.

Eric began breaking through the lavatory door, and other passengers gathered beside him. All kinds of yelling came from every direction. I looked toward the back of the plane, where Eric's foot had broken through the lavatory door, back to the flight attendants, who had taken position between me and the cockpit. They had formed their barricade and were gripping knives in their hands. No effing joke, they had knives, and they meant business.

In the meantime, the plane could only circle Los Angeles. About twenty minutes went by, though if you'd have asked me, I would have said it had been about twenty seconds.

Eric was finally able to pull the door completely open, and he and several passengers grabbed the lunatic and yanked him out. Smoke billowed from the lavatory as they threw him to the ground and subdued him. The man started screaming, "There's a bomb on the plane! There's a bomb on the plane!"

"Shut the fuck up!" Eric yelled. However, this guy was so psychotic, he just kept screaming. They had him pinned down but were still fighting to keep him under control.

At this point, I noticed that we were no longer circling LA. Instead, we were heading out over the Pacific Ocean. The pilot's voice crackled over the PA system, "I have control of the aircraft, but air-traffic control has instructed us to wait in a holding pattern." Just as he said that, a roaring sound caught my attention outside my window. What I saw turned me as white as a set of 1,500-thread-count Egyptian-cotton sheets: two F-15 fighter jets.

I slumped into my seat. "Oh, fuck," I said.

I was seated so close to our plane's cockpit that as I looked out the window, I could see the lead fighter pilot's face. He pulled his plane forward until he was across from our captain, and they began to communicate with one another. I mean, the fighter pilot was wearing an oxygen mask, but the rest of his face, including his eyes, were completely visible to me. He looked pale . . . really pale.

Everything flooded over me. *Rules of engagement.* That's what the secretary of defense had been talking about. The military had been instructed that if another plane was hijacked, rather than let it crash into a building full of people, they were to shoot it down. The F-15 pilot looked like he was scared shitless, terrified of what he was supposed to do. But, he was going to shoot us down if he had to.

Finally, our pilot came on the intercom to inform us that LAX was not going to let us land. He said, "If we do have a bomb onboard, and it detonated over a populated area, a huge number of people on the ground would be killed. They aren't even allowing us into their airspace."

At this point, we were approaching international waters, which meant this wasn't just a United States problem. And, since this was a Canadian airline, it was a Canadian problem, too.

All of us passengers were really scared, and a couple of people began to cry. The captain told us the US government was trying to get the Canadian prime minister on the phone so they could get permission from the Canadians to shoot us down. The captain actually told us that, and when he did, my mouth hung open so wide that I was certain my jaw would fall off.

Then, the pilot unlocked the cockpit door and came out to face us. I think he wanted to show us all that he was a real person in control of the plane, and he was going to do everything in his power to get us out of this. He let us know that the smoldering fire in the lavatory had been extinguished. Of course, the cabin was still filled with smoke and the terrorist asshole was still screaming. But, with Eric and several other passengers sitting on his back, he wasn't going anywhere.

Anyway, the captain went on to tell us that the air-traffic controllers said we could not return. He then said that we had two choices. We could comply with the holding pattern and let them shoot us down, if necessary. Or, we could try to force a landing at LAX, potentially killing a bunch of people if a bomb were to detonate.

"We're all from democratic societies," he said. "So, let's take a vote. What do we do?"

Everyone got really quiet. Then, about 90 percent of the people voted that we should let them shoot us down rather than risk killing a bunch of people on the ground. The pilot swallowed. "Okay," he finally said. "I'm going to call my wife, and then we're going to do what we have to do. God bless us all."

I called my mother again. She said, "What's going on now?"

I was trying to stay calm. "Before we boarded, I heard an announcement that the government had invoked 'the rules of engagement,' instructing the US Air Force to shoot down hijacked planes like ours. I want you to be prepared."

She became hysterical. Tears streamed down my face.

At that point, we saw the F-15s pull back, taking up position behind us. We now all knew, *This is it. They're going to shoot us down. We're going to die.*

A few minutes later, the pilot assured us he'd get back on the intercom before they were to shoot us down. For now, however, there was nothing else we could do. The cabin of the plane fell silent. Even the terrorist finally shut up. People cried quietly. Those with loved ones hugged each other and held hands. All we could hear was the constant drone of the engines. We sat and waited, certain that a missile, fired from one of the F-15s, would slam into us at any moment.

While other passengers kept the terrorist under control, Eric came back up, sat in his seat, and called his wife. I heard him explain things to her. He told her he loved her, and they talked for several minutes. Then he sat there, choking back tears while I openly wept. He was strong. Stronger than me. Plus, he had had the guts to face down a terrorist head on.

Unbeknownst to us, authorities were still trying to get Canada's prime minister on the phone, but he was in a closed session in Ottawa. Fortunately for us, they still didn't have permission to shoot our plane down.

We heard a clicking sound as the PA system once again crackled to life. *This is it,* I thought. *This will be the announcement from the captain that we're about to die.* "Ladies and gentlemen, this is the captain. I've just got off the comm with LAX. They're going to give us one chance."

"What?" I said, my voice frantic.

"If we do it right now, they'll let us attempt a speed-landing on runway niner-six, a remote runway."

My mouth gaped open, but no sounds emerged.

He continued, "Flight attendants, prepare the cabin for an emergency landing."

Within seconds, flight attendants swarmed the aisles yelling instructions. "Everyone, we're going to assume crash positions. Check that your seat belt is securely fastened. Lean forward with your feet flat on floor. Place your head facedown into your lap. Wrap your arms under your knees. Do it now!"

I could barely move. I was frozen, scared shitless, but Eric tapped me on the shoulder to snap me out of it. I got into the position. The pilot must have been a fighter jock in his younger days, because he wrenched the plane into a hard left turn, even harder than the one we did earlier, and we dropped out of the sky like a rock. He whipped the son of a bitch over a runway and then jammed us down onto the pavement.

Man, we hit down hard . . . really hard. I mean, everybody's hearts were in their throats. I didn't even know if we were going to survive the landing, because we must have been going at least three hundred miles per hour as we slammed down. I popped my head up and looked out the windows to see a swarm of firetrucks, police vehicles, and ambulances rocketing down the runway with us. There must have been a hundred of them.

The plane jostled and swerved as it slowed down. The pilot veered us off the runway and into a field. Seriously, we were now bumping across the grassy, marshlike area adjacent to LAX. As we came to a stop, we heard several helicopters overhead. They circled the plane once, then landed, one at the nose of the plane, the other at the tail. Out of the helicopters, SWAT guys (or FBI guys, or Army stormtroopers, or something) jumped out and came running toward the plane. They had facemasks in place, automatic weapons in hand. At least twenty-five rushed onto the plane with their rifles pointed at us, screaming, "Everybody, facedown on the floor!"

I barely had time to move before one of them grabbed me by the back of the neck and shoved me onto the floor, right next to this woman. Her face and mine were only inches apart, and in the midst of all this terror and yelling, I said, "Don't they ever clean the fucking floors?" She probably thought I was a nutjob.

These guys were total professionals operating in a state of controlled panic, as they believed there was a bomb onboard. Several rushed to the back, where they tackled the crap out of the terrorist. They handcuffed him and wrestled him to the rear door. Then, they tossed him out of the plane. I mean, literally, they popped open one of the emergency doors and dropped him about thirty feet to the ground. They didn't give a damn about him, and I didn't blame them. Next, they deployed all of the evacuation slides and rushed us back to our feet.

There was a melee of people all clamoring to get out, but the SWAT team guys pretty much kept everyone in check. They deplaned us in reverse order, with the passengers seated closest to the terrorist in the back out first. Because Eric and I were seated in first class 1A and 1B, we were the last passengers down the slide. I was followed by the flight attendants. I looked back up into the open door and could see the pilot arguing with the stormtroopers. Over the thumping of the helicopter rotors and the plane engines still cycling down, I heard him yell, "The captain is the last to leave. Now, get off my goddamned flight deck!" He was old-school, a tough man. He had saved our lives, and he was right: the captain *is* the last to leave. But, they weren't having any of it. He jumped onto the slide, and we ran clear of the plane with the stormtroopers right behind us.

By this point, all of the passenger busses had already departed. So, all of us remaining—Eric, the pilot, the flight attendants, and myself—jumped into the back of a truck. As they drove us away, I turned and looked back. The sight was surreal: a ton of police vehicles, blue lights blazing, all surrounding a Boeing 737 parked in the middle of the marsh.

As much as I hate to say it, that wasn't the end of the story.

FLIGHT OF THE DAMNED

All of us were herded into this holding area somewhere in the bowels of LAX. I'm talking about *everybody*—the passengers, the pilots, the flight attendants, the whole lot. It felt like we were in a dungeon or something. Everyone tried to calm down, but we were given instructions not to talk to one another or use our cell phones.

We sat there for two or three hours. We weren't given any information. We weren't allowed to call our families. We had no access to water, food, or bathrooms. Nothing.

Finally, the authorities informed us they would be questioning each of us one by one in the order we had deplaned. Our interrogation, as I like to call it, lasted about fifteen minutes each. As I sat there waiting for my turn, I couldn't help but think, *My family probably has no information about me at all. They don't even know if I'm alive or dead.*

As each person emerged from their interrogation, their faces looked awash with shock. It was intimidating as hell. I sell beauty products, for God's sake. I'm not cut out for this shit! I figured, *Look, just calm down. Once they've questioned you, I'm sure you'll be free to go.* Don't I wish that had been true.

When my name was finally called, I got up and was led through a door. It turned out that the door led to an underground driveway of sorts. The men in charge loaded me into a truck, and we drove outside. "Where are we going?" I asked. No answer.

By this time, hours had elapsed, and they'd determined that there was no bomb on the plane. So, they drove on a side road around the edge of the airport before crossing back into the airport fence line. I could see our aircraft in the distance, still parked in the same spot. They instructed me to board the plane and pick up my carry-on bag. Afterward, I was driven right back to the underground dungeon, where the questioning began.

Two men started rifling through my bag. After they finished, one ordered, "Take off your clothes."

"What?"

"We have to search you. Now, strip."

Holy shit! "Where do you think we are? Riyadh?" I asked. Believe me, that statement did not go over well. I took off my clothes and they performed a complete body search. I *won't* go into the details, but it wasn't pleasant, I assure you. "Am I free to go now?" I said.

"Not quite," the man answered. "Get dressed. There's a little matter we need to discuss with you."

My head reeled. *"A little matter"? What the fuck is he talking about?* I thought to myself. I was dying to say, "Oh, you want to talk business? Is that it? Perhaps you'd like to open up your own white-labeled line of cosmetics? You know, I can help with that." But for once, I kept my mouth closed.

"We need to discuss your visa."

"My visa? What about it?"

He sat behind a table and studied some papers. "We find it very interesting that you've got a visa granting you access to Egypt. That's not that far from Palestine."

"Palestine? What's Palestine got to do with anything?"

"The terrorist on your flight was from Palestine."

The fact that I had made travel plans to a Middle Eastern country a few weeks prior hadn't even crossed my mind. I mean, why would it? I told the investigators the whole story: the Dubai trade show, that I had left LA, but the flight had been diverted to Phoenix.

They didn't believe me.

So, now these guys thought that I was somehow involved. Yeah, sure, a "cosmetic baron" tried to blow up a plane with his stash of face cream. Happens all the time.

The interrogation continued, but by this point I was beginning to get a little fed up. "I can just see it," I said. "Maybe I'll try to take down an airliner with a nice rouge and maybe some eyeliner." They didn't think that was funny, either.

Finally, they let me go. At that point, I was taken to another room where, to my surprise, about three hundred people were seated. It was all of the passengers. This was, like, ten hours later, and I couldn't believe my eyes. They were all still here!

Not long thereafter, two government agents came out. One announced, "You can't go home yet. We're going to need you to complete your itinerary."

"What the fuck?" I said.

"You can't speak of this event to *anyone* until you get the okay from us."

Again, "What the fuck?"

"We need you to get back on the aircraft. You'll be heading to Toronto as if nothing ever happened. It will be like the plane was simply delayed."

I was baffled, absolutely baffled. Our flight had originally been scheduled to depart at 7:40 a.m. I muttered under my breath, "It's now eleven thirty at night, and you jackasses want us to pretend we didn't almost just die, and to just go about our merry way to Toronto?"

We were driven out to a new plane with a totally new flight crew. The plane had been towed back onto the runway, and we were assigned the same seats we'd had on the potentially doomed plane. It was like being in an episode of *The Twilight Zone*. By now, almost twenty hours had gone by, and we still hadn't had any food or water. The first time we saw those things was when we reboarded the aircraft.

The new flight crew knew a major incident had occurred, but they didn't know we were the group of passengers that had been on board that plane. They had absolutely no clue what we'd been through. They walked down the aisles welcoming us with big smiles on their faces, and we were so weary and disheveled, we must have looked insane. In fact, we must have looked like the flight of the damned.

Upon takeoff, I really started to wonder what was going on. As part of an apparent cover-up by authorities, they flew us from LAX to San Francisco, to Dallas, back to San Francisco, then to Chicago, Atlanta, Miami, back to San Francisco, and finally, on to Toronto. They stopped, of course, to fuel up in between, but wouldn't let us off. I shit you not. That's what happened. They must have been trying to account for all the time that our plane was off the grid or something.

When we finally landed in Toronto, I was the first one off the plane, and if I never have another flight, that's fine with me. It had been such a long ordeal, I was actually growing facial hair. Starving and crazy-tired, I walked into the terminal, where a sea of media cameras and bright lights burst into my face. There were reporters everywhere going berserk. "What happened?" they kept yelling. "What's going on? What was the delay?" There had been so much secrecy and disinformation spread by both the US and Canadian governments that reporters still didn't have the full story. They didn't know our plane was the one that had been involved in the incident. At this point, all they knew was that our flight was over twenty-four hours late for its arrival in Toronto, and no one would tell them why.

I just kept walking and said, "It was a really long trip."

Closing the Deal

J ust when you thought it was safe to go back in the water . . . oh, no, no! The trip from hell wasn't over yet.

I had an important business meeting with a buyer, which is why I had traveled to Canada in the first place. The buyer was in Guelph, a small town in southwestern Ontario roughly sixty miles west of Toronto. In my exhaustion after the plane debacle, I was really confused about what day it was, much less the time of day. Could I make it to my meeting on time? Had I missed it?

Immediately upon leaving the Toronto airport, I asked my driver for the time and had him drive me straight to Guelph. Like I said, it's about sixty miles away, so it took a while. It was only after we arrived that I caught a glimpse of my reflection. I looked like a madman: my hair was all over the place, I hadn't shaved, my eyes were beet-red, and my clothes were wrinkled and dirty.

Once I got inside, I was escorted into a big meeting room full of people. All of these businessmen looked startled at my appearance. One asked me, "What happened to you?" But, of course, I couldn't tell them. I just had to play it off like it had simply been a long trip.

I don't know how I was able to do it, but somehow I closed a $25,000 deal. I mean, I was nearly catatonic from a lack of sleep, but I was able to close the deal anyway. I was proud of myself.

I stumbled out of there and into the waiting town car. Finally, I was headed to my hotel. All I could think of was falling face first onto the bed. I was exhausted. As soon as I got checked in, I gorged myself for about twenty minutes. My eyes were literally burning from lack of sleep, but I hadn't eaten in more than a day and was absolutely starved. After my ordeal, everything tasted like fine caviar.

Before you start feeling relieved that I was finally about to get my much overdue rest, wait until you hear this. After letting my freaked-out mother know that I had indeed survived my ordeal, I collapsed onto the bed, but it couldn't have been thirty seconds later that I heard this insanely loud blaring. I sat bolt-upright in my bed and covered my ears. "What the hell is that?" As it turned out, it was a fire alarm. In the midst of the blaring sound, a voice came over the speaker and said, "Ladies and gentlemen, we're sorry to interrupt you, but at this time we are asking all guests to please evacuate the building. Please evacuate immediately."

I said out loud, "I don't give a fuck if I burn! I'm not moving."

Since I literally hadn't bathed in days and couldn't sleep with the incessant noise, anyway, I went into the bathroom and filled the tub with hot water. All the while, the alarm still raised hell. I got in the bathtub, put my head under the water so I couldn't hear the friggin' siren, and held my breath as long as I could. When I finally came back up, the siren, blessedly, had stopped.

I toweled off and climbed into bed, and I don't think I woke up for about fourteen hours. Oh, and you're going to love it when you find out what the alarm was about. It turns out that there was a terrorist scare at my hotel. Some nutjob had called in to say he was going to blow the building up. I was in abject shock upon hearing that. What are the odds to be in two terrorist scares back to back? Unbelievable!

I tried to slow down over the next three or four days as I wrapped up my meetings. My sales trip to Canada finally ended, and I was happy because I had closed deals for a crap-ton of beauty products. Those beauty products would later make the Canadian people more beautiful than they already are.

I headed off to the airport. Little did I know, authorities had put me on a *terror watch list*. Me, Vinny, the guy with a carry-on bag full of eyeliner and hand cream. It was all because of the trip to Dubai with a stopover in Egypt I had planned. Hell, if I would have known that traveling in the Middle East would be that much trouble, I wouldn't have booked the trip in the first place.

When I got to the airport, a Canadian Mountie said, "What are you doing here?"

"Huh?" I replied.

"What was your business in Canada?" he barked.

"Well, my company is Natural Cosmetics. We're based in Los

Angeles. We sell skincare, haircare, and bath and beauty products. It was a business trip."

"That sounds like a load of crap. You will not be boarding a flight."

"What are you talking about? I'm an American citizen. I'm going back to America. I'm just here on business," I insisted, but this guy would have none of it. *What an asshole*, I thought. Out loud I said, "Why can't I board the plane?"

The Mounties ended up calling my boss at Natural Cosmetics to tell him I would not be able to leave Canada unless my story checked out. They told Chuck to fax my employment contract to them. After they received it, they called the Egyptian consulate in San Francisco. The consulate had to go through their records to look me up, and finally confirmed what I had already told the Canadian authorities about my planned business trip to Dubai.

So now, even though my employment checked out, I had a US passport, and the consulates in Dubai and Egypt confirmed exactly what I had told them, the Mounties wanted a birth certificate.

"Wait, now you want a birth certificate?" I questioned. "Do you think I travel around with a copy of my birth certificate on me?"

The guy just sat there stone-faced as he stared back at me. He was actually waiting for me to produce a birth certificate. He said, "No birth certificate, no flight."

My mouth dropped open. I mean, I was standing there with my bags in one hand and a boarding ticket in the other. But, the angry Canadian wasn't going to let me through. I had no choice. I had to get a copy of my birth certificate. So, I called my mom. The poor woman had practically been worried to death over me, and now she had to put up with this? Let me tell you something. Had she been with me, she probably would have broken that Canadian Mountie's jaw.

I was stuck for another night in Canada, and Mom had to drive forty-five miles into Philadelphia to the hospital where I was born to get the records. She faxed a copy directly from the hospital, but, oh no, that wasn't good enough.

"This faxed copy won't do," the jerk said. "Come back when you have a hard copy. Then, maybe we'll talk."

I couldn't believe it! My already fragile nerves were wearing thin. I retreated back to the posh confines of my hotel to wait it out for another night. My mother had to overnight a hard copy. When it arrived the next morning, I went back to what was fast becoming my least favorite place: the airport.

This time, they couldn't find any other stupid reason to detain me, so I was allowed to board like a normal person. I got on the plane, took my seat in first class, and proceeded to cry like a little schoolgirl. It had all been too much. I was mentally and physically exhausted.

I learned later that had we been flying on a US carrier when the terrorist tried to take our plane down, we would have been shot down without hesitation. Sitting there on the plane, I finally had time to think about it, and I realized how close I had come to death. The experience made my hair stand on end—not that a guy with trichotillomania has much hair, mind you.

If that whole story were ever told, like in a book or something, you'd probably say it couldn't be true. Only, it was.

Misadventures Mayhem

As my time with Natural Cosmetics wound down, my next trip was to go shut up one of the company's brokers. Well, *shut up* is kind of harsh. It was more like *appease.* This broker had been complaining of late that no one from our corporate office ever visited them. Their office was located in Halifax, Nova-freaking-Scotia. *Well, no wonder no one ever visits you,* I thought. *You live in Nova Scotia, for God's sake. It's a frozen block of ice most of the year.*

Anyway, I kicked off my "Frozen Tour" and grabbed a flight. After landing and getting off the plane into negative-twenty-degree weather, I found out that our rep there had quit without telling anyone. Yeah, he had quit. So, here I was outside the airport, standing like an idiot in the middle of the frozen tundra, with no one to pick me up because no one knew the guy had quit. Oh, well. So much for the Frozen Tour.

The next stop was Montreal, where I had an equally cold experience, albeit a bit messier. I knew our rep there was a very classy lady. I could just picture it. When she came to the airport to pick me up, she would be dressed to the nines, dazzling in furs. Well, our plane set down in a crazy blizzard. In fact, there was so much snow, they weren't even able to pull the jet up to the gate. They made us get out onto the runway.

So, in keeping with our classy sales rep, I was dressed in this gorgeous virgin-white Armani snow outfit that I had gotten especially for the trip. I figured it would be a great fashion statement to show up in. I mean, this outfit was beautiful. Imagine my horror when, as I walked down the stairs from the plane, I slipped and my feet went straight up in the air. It all seemed to happen in slow motion. I have this distinct image in my mind from that day, and it's of my feet silhouetted against the sky. I came crashing down on my back in a pile of snow muck—all slush and dirt. It knocked the wind out of me, and my fabulous outfit was completely ruined.

Watching that happen from a distance must have been hilarious, but like I said, the sales rep waiting for me was a classy lady, and she didn't bat an eye. But, if you think that's the only travel misadventure I had on this "farewell journey" for Natural Cosmetics, you'd be wrong. You'd be way wrong. I was just getting warmed up.

I decided I'd had enough of the frozen North. My next trip for Natural Cosmetics took me in the opposite direction. I traveled way down south, all the way to Orlando, Florida. There was a big beauty industry trade show about to happen there, and I had long been registered to attend. I wanted to be there for myself to shake hands and make connections that would help me in the future.

As was my custom, I booked a very posh hotel. It was decked out in fake safari stuff, like full-sized elephants, lions, tigers, and those antelope-looking things with huge pointy horns. The interior of the hotel was covered in tropical foliage. I'm talking about trees and plants everywhere, and it even had a stream running through the lobby. I mean, this place actually had its own zoo! The whole place was a bit surreal, but being as close as it was to the Disney and Universal theme parks, it fit right in.

So began another one of my epic adventures. Unfortunately, the scale of embarrassment of this one made my slip-and-fall in Montreal look like child's play.

On this particular day, I had free time. My work on the trade-show floor had been a huge success, what with meeting buyers, making new connections, and closing sales for Natural Cosmetics. Now, it was time for a day off.

Naturally, I decided to go hang out by the pool. The pool itself was gargantuan, surrounded by palm trees and tropical foliage of all types. They even had two or three water slides for both kids and adults. These slides were the enclosed type, built as tubes with water rushing down them. Man, they looked like so much fun! After a while of sitting there in my fabulous new Burberry bathing suit, I decided I had to give it a try. After all, this was my day off, and I deserved a little fun.

I walked over to the slides and ascended the stairs. Upon reaching the top, I hopped in. I started slip-sliding down, but then my body's momentum stopped, and I heard this hideous ripping sound. I was stuck! Unbeknownst to me, I had gone down the kid's slide.

Oh, shit!

This thing was too small for me. I had one arm stuck over my head, one arm pinned to my side, and water was rushing all around me. I couldn't move! I was seriously uncomfortable and could hear all the kids laughing. Three or four minutes went by, and even though I wiggled and squirmed, I soon realized I couldn't get out. I mean, I was totally jammed in there! Through a window in the tube, I could see the kids standing on the staircase not ten feet from me. I yelled through the tube to them, "You've got to go get some help! I'm stuck in here and can't get out."

They laughed harder but scurried down the steps to get a lifeguard. A minute later, the lifeguard came up. "Hey, are you really stuck?"

"No, dipwad, I just thought I'd hold myself inside a tube of rushing water for a while." Well, okay, I didn't really tell him that. Needless to say, the guy could see I was wedged in there. He pondered the situation for a minute and then, in his brilliant wisdom, came up with an idea. "I'll just turn on the water really hard. We'll have you flushed out of there in no time!" he yelled.

He ran off and turned the water pressure up full blast before I could say, "No! Don't do that. I might drown, you idiot!" Now there was so much water rushing over me, it was getting in my face, and I began having trouble breathing. I craned my neck to keep my mouth in the clear so I could breathe, but I certainly wasn't budging. I mean, I was really jammed in there tight.

Remember that ripping sound when I first got stuck? Well, as it turns out, that was my bathing suit. My *new* Burberry bathing suit. It ripped right off me. At this point, though, I don't think anyone could tell that I was naked.

I started yelling as loud as I could, but over the noise of the rushing water, nobody could hear me. Finally, they turned the water pressure way down again, and I could now see that a crowd of about fifty people had gathered.

The lifeguard then had another one of his epiphanies. He got one of the bigger kids to get into the tube, and he held the kid's hand to keep him from going down. The kid was just far enough into the tube that he could push against my shoulders with his feet. Well, that didn't work, and people began laughing. They were having a grand old time at my expense. No one was taking this seriously, including the lifeguard.

This went on for about forty-five minutes, and by this point, I was getting really hot inside the tube. Meanwhile, in another brilliant idea, the lifeguard got a tub of melted butter from a nearby popcorn machine. He then proceeded to pour it down the slide until I was absolutely coated in the stuff. In all the heat, I felt like a Thanksgiving turkey. Suffice to say, I was still stuck.

Finally, about an hour and a half into this thing, a crew of firefighters showed up. *I'm saved*, I thought. At this point, I was really starting to hurt.

Well, even the firefighters had a hard time keeping a straight face. Just picture it: you're a firefighter, and you show up to find a naked Italian man, covered in butter, wedged into a water slide. I mean, you just can't make this stuff up.

One firefighter lowered down a little camera on a scope so he could get a better look. He called down to me, "Wait a minute. Are you really naked?"

"Yes!" I said.

"Are you covered in butter?"

"No, I just really liked the buttered popcorn."

He didn't think that was funny. They decided to try the water pressure again, but instead of using water from the slide, they turned the fire hose on me. I started yelling, "No, no, no!" God, the idiots could have drowned me.

It's then that I noticed a news crew from a local Orlando TV station had shown up. I was beyond horrified. What I didn't know was that this was being broadcast on the local news channel, and people all over the trade-show floor were tuning in. These were all my customers, distributors, vendors, and colleagues. They were literally watching this thing unfold on TV, but they didn't know it was me.

The hotel manager finally came out, and I overheard the fire chief telling him that they were going to have to cut me out of the slide. There was a brief argument, but the firefighters were going to do what they had to do to get me out. Soon, they asked me to tap the side of the tube with my feet so they could be sure they knew where they were. That way, when they began cutting, they wouldn't cut my feet off. They let the power saw rip, and a few minutes later, a big chunk of the slide popped out, providing an opening. Two of the firemen pulled me out by my feet.

Having been jammed in like that for so long was really painful. When I finally popped out, I felt like I was paralyzed. I was sore, raw, and could barely get my arm down from above my head, much less stand upright. The firefighters helped me.

People in the crowd started pointing and snickering. Then someone yelled, "Oh, my God. He's naked!" The laughter erupted.

Meanwhile, on the trade-show floor, my colleagues stared at the television monitors. As I was pulled out, they all said, "Oh, my God, it's Vince!"

When it was all said and done, I had been stuck in that tube for over two hours. Naked. Covered in butter.

The following morning at the trade show, I walked through the massive double doors at the entrance. Over the loudspeaker I heard a voice announce, "Well, Vince is here, everybody, the buttered-rum baby!" I tried to take it in stride. I mean, what else could I do? It had been very traumatic and painful, but in retrospect, it must have looked pretty damned funny.

Three months later, I got a bill from the hotel. They wanted me to pay $30,000, stating that I had ruined their water slide. However, when I mentioned to them that there was no signage warning that these slides were too small for adults, they quieted down. Needless to say, they've never seen a dime of my money.

Vinny to the Rescue

Whenever I wasn't on the road for Natural Cosmetics, I socialized in LA, but I mostly thought about Rob. He lived in New York at this point, but would come out to see me periodically. As was always the case with Rob, we were never physical together. He never wanted to sleep with me. I was (still) out-of-control in love with him, but he (still) didn't feel the same way. Due to my obsession with him, I had been paying for his college tuition for years, even though there were times I couldn't afford it.

Unfortunately, he was still using drugs, which was *so* not me. I didn't really drink, I never tried pot, and I never tried blow. And, if you want to know the truth, I never even smoked a cigarette.

Unfortunately, during those first years that I lived in California, Rob, the man who had become the obsession of my life, did.

If I had to describe myself at that time, I'd say it was like living a Jekyll-and-Hyde lifestyle. I was two people. One, a hardworking professional who was going to be successful, even if it killed him; the other, a man obsessed with someone who didn't feel the same way. The truth was, even during the working day, I was thinking about Rob. I may not have ever used drugs, but *Rob* was my drug.

One summer, Rob moved out to LA. Now, up until this point, as far as I knew, his drug use had been mainly recreational. You know, a little pot here, an ecstasy tablet there . . . or so I thought. This just goes to show how totally clueless I was where Rob was concerned.

When he moved to California, his drug use escalated. Rob's personality had always been a little unstable, but he had done fairly well as a college student, and I thought he was getting along reasonably well. It wasn't until much later that I learned he had never graduated. He had quit with only two classes to go. So, my "investment" in his education went down the tube like so many other things in my life.

The California lifestyle just overtook him. Cali is a place that can either get into your blood, or if you let it, *take* your blood. In Rob's case, he just didn't have any self-control. California will kill you for that. He told me he felt free to push the envelope because he had been brutally molested by a straight uncle on his dad's side when he first came out as a teenager. He said it was his way of getting even, though I never figured out the rationalization.

While he was crashing at my place, I would go to work, just like anybody would, and Rob would sleep the entire day. Then, he would wake up at night and come alive. The problem was, he didn't want to be with me. He didn't want to hang out with my friends. The more he rejected me, though, the more I wanted him.

With all this far, far behind me now, it's almost embarrassing talking about it. I've become a respected businessman, but I believe it's important that each of us face our past.

I rolled right back into my old habits of treating Rob lavishly. I went to great efforts and spent a lot of money getting him situated in my apartment. I bought him designer clothes. I helped him pay off his car. But at night, I didn't know what he was doing. He would disappear and not show up until the early-morning hours. It killed me.

Yes, I was nuts for putting up with his crap, but I was in love. The situation only got steadily worse . . . much worse. Rob was really good at hiding and lying, and back then, I was so naïve, I was literally blind to it. All my friends knew that Rob was bad news. They knew he was having an affair with another man, but I steadfastly refused to believe what they tried to tell me. They also knew the other man was a male prostitute. Yep, that's right. Rob was dating a guy who was paid to have sex with other men. In the world of drugs and AIDS, it doesn't get more dangerous than that.

Around this time, I started losing friends and Rob started going deeper into the drug world. The deeper he went into drugs, the deeper I got into him. He was pulling further and further away, and I wanted to pull him back.

The guy he was dating was named Trent. Not only was Trent a male prostitute into drugs, he was also a great salesman. He convinced Rob to come into the escort business with him. So, Rob went from a pot-smoking New York college student to snorting coke on a daily basis. He and Trent also began cooking something they called "Special K."

Now, like I said, I didn't do drugs, so I didn't even know what Special K was. But, I learned. It was a popular recreational drug in the LA club scene. It's basically an illicit version of the drug ketamine, a medication used for anesthesia. It induces a trancelike state and makes you feel like you are pain-free. It also has this interesting side effect of making a depressed person feel much better. I guess I can see the appeal, but all those euphoric effects have a dark side. The drug commonly causes hallucinations, and that's what I think happened to Rob next.

He and I began getting into bad arguments. It was as if I didn't know who he was anymore. In his rage, he would fly off the handle and end up yelling at me like a lunatic. Then, things turned really ugly. Late one night, the phone rang. It was Rob. I sat bolt-upright in bed. "What's wrong?" I blurted in a sudden state of alertness.

"Me and Trent got arrested," he said with a bit of a slur to his words.

Despite all the warnings from my friends, I still refused to believe just how bad Rob really was for me. Looking back, it was insane. I was insane. He had even gone to the point of making sure all his friends knew that they needed to be careful of what they said around me. He had told them I was his meal ticket, and he didn't want to screw that up. *A meal ticket.* That's all I meant to him? He only wanted me for money? I hate to admit that I still wasn't ready to believe just how sick my obsession was.

His call sent my heart rate through the roof.

"Vinny," he pleaded, "you've got to come get me out of here."

"What happened?" I said. "Why did you get arrested?"

I thought for sure he was going to say that it was for drug

possession, but he didn't. He began blubbering into the phone. I could barely understand him. "They charged us with domestic violence."

"Us? You mean you and Trent? Domestic vio—" I couldn't spit out another syllable. My throat choked shut as I was overcome with emotion. The truth had hit me squarely between the eyes. They weren't just hanging out together, they weren't just dating; they were lovers so intertwined with each other that they were having violent arguments. Everything my friends had said was true, and it all came crashing down over me.

Even so, I went down to the jail. It made no sense, but I did it. Vinny to the rescue again. I was so batshit crazy over Rob that I kept thinking I could change him and make him love me. Like I said, batshit crazy.

In order to get him out of jail, I had to secure a bail bond. I barely knew what a bail bond was. Now, I don't recall how much his bail was set at, but I do remember that in California, you have to put down 10 percent of your own money to get a bond. In order to secure this one, I had to leverage everything I had. It even came down to me having to hawk some of my belongings to raise the cash. The entire process took ten hours, and I was emotionally exhausted. When Rob walked out of jail, he hugged me and cried. Then he said something that almost made me vomit: "We have to get Trent out."

My shoulders slumped. Hearing those words hurt. But, I did what any good Vinny would do: I bailed Trent out, too.

My obsession with Rob lived on.

It's in the Blood

Despite all the chaos in my home life, I was somehow still able to focus on the beauty business. After fulfilling my forty-five-day notice, I departed Natural Cosmetics and headed out to find the next great adventure in my quest for business success. I also began to realize something. I was an entrepreneur. I mean, I was *really* an entrepreneur. I don't know why it took so long for it to hit home, but once it did, it became obvious. Entrepreneurialism was somehow in my blood.

I can work with people really easily, but I can't answer to them. I can do things my way, but not someone else's. I can conform to what I know I need to do, but can never conform to what people are telling me to do. I can create my own schedule, but I can't operate on other people's. That might make me sound like an ass, but it's not that. I'm a tremendous collaborator. I love people. I love creating. I love the business I lead today.

Sadly, I just wasn't financially ready to step out on my own yet.

I sucked it up and went to work next at a company that we'll call "US Industries." It's not a pretty name, but they made pretty products. All the beauty products they manufactured were private label. They were smack dab in the middle of what I wanted to do, and they were talking my language.

Even today, this company is large. They develop and manufacture a large percentage of what customers buy at the famous Sally Beauty Supply. It doesn't matter what the label says; if it's sold at Sally, the product was probably manufactured by US Industries.

Sally has about fifteen different brands, most of them in the skincare market. Their big thing, though, is reverse-engineering. Reverse-engineering is when you take an entire beauty product apart, and analyze it to see what elements it contains and in what quantities. Then, you essentially make a copy, but add a slight twist to the ingredients, and sell it under your own name.

As a client, Sally execs would come to me and let me know that they had their sights set on a particular product. For example, let's say it was a jar of Helena Rubinstein face cream. Keep in mind, Helena Rubinstein goes for around $350 a jar. In other words, it ain't cheap, and it ain't crap. The Sally execs would want us to reverse-engineer the product and then manufacture a knock-off for them, all at a wholesale cost of around three bucks a bottle. Now, when you compare three dollars a bottle to three hundred, it might not sound like you'd be earning much money. However, when you scale it into huge volume, it ends up being a crap-ton of money for US Industries (and a nice, fat commission check for Vinny).

Again, with US Industries, I got to be in the lab. Working side by side with the chemist, I was able to learn how to actually put the product together. Benching a product is always so fascinating for me. I loved it. In this case, since I already had a little benching experience, they let me do it.

There's always a master chemist in the lab who oversees all the other bench chemists, and when I got stuck, I could always ask him a question. A lot of the time I would shadow the guy and just learn. It was like working in a lab full of entrepreneurs. We were all engrossed in our work.

Yet, there was a downside. Because there was so little real supervision, you could be working on something for three months, and then be told that it was all wrong. Man, that really sucked. You would have to redo the whole thing, which is both ridiculous and time wasting. On the other hand, I was free to learn whatever I wanted.

I was really enjoying my time at this place, but in true Vinny fashion, my entrepreneurial bug would pop out at any point along the way and bite me. As I said before, I have a really hard time answering to people. I want to do what I want to do. So, my insubordination, as usual, was in overdrive. It wasn't until they installed a time clock that I had really had enough. I mean, think about it—a time clock! What is this, 1978? Had I wanted to work at a place with a time clock, I would have stayed in Jersey and joined my local plumbers union. That was the end of the line at US Industries for me. Not a very bright move, considering I didn't have another job lined up.

P.S. If you are a plumber, don't hate me. It's just an example. Then again, if you are a plumber, why are you reading this book?

Oh, Rob

Right about that time, Rob's drug use escalated even further, and his behavior shifted. I began noticing tics, like excessive blinking and twitching. Then, he started mumbling under his breath.

"Rob, what's going on? You're twitching and talking to yourself."

"What are you talking about?" he would reply. He had no idea he was even doing it, and it only became progressively worse. That's when I learned about Tina, someone else who had entered his life. Let me tell you something: Tina was a real bitch. But, before you start wondering whether Rob had "switched teams," you have to know who Tina is.

At the time in LA, many gay men had started getting into a drug, a really hard-core drug, called crystal methamphetamine. Crystal meth had become *the* party/sex drug of choice. On the street, it was known as "Tina." Its use results in a high that numbs your senses and causes hyperactivity. It also increases stamina, allowing a person to party for long periods of time. With all that euphoria comes a marked reduction in inhibitions.

People high on meth don't care about much of anything. They're not worried about the dangers of their behavior, they're not worried about their health, and they damn sure aren't worried about contracting HIV from unprotected sex. It became, and still is, a wrecking ball in the gay community.

There were times when I'd watch Rob have a full conversation with nobody. He'd laugh and giggle, but then start arguing with himself. His hands would flail in the air as he sat on the balcony chain-smoking and talking to this person who was not there. Of course, this behavior started to freak me out, because he was actually becoming violent.

I got so worried, I couldn't sleep anymore. It affected my work life. In fact, it was affecting every area of my life. I was *always* worried about Rob, and I finally came to my senses. Rob was dangerous, and I had to get him out of my apartment.

It makes no sense to me now, but instead of kicking him to the curb or buying him a one-way ticket to New Jersey, I got him his own place: an apartment out in Sherman Oaks. As you might imagine, I paid the rent. In true Rob fashion, he repented and said he was going to get a regular job and everything would be okay. Well, that was crap, and I think I knew it.

He only lived in that apartment for about two months. During that time period, he would still come visit me. The problem was, I would come home from work to find something wrong in my apartment. My computer would be in parts spread out all over the floor, or Rob would be there, passed out. He was becoming more and more paranoid by the day, always looking behind himself. He thought he was being followed.

Another time, one of the neighbors at his apartment called me. She said they could hear screaming coming from Rob's place. I drove over there and found that he was inside, alone, just screaming his head off. It was bonkers. But, it was toward the end of his stay there that it hit me just how bad things had become.

Sometime later, no one, including me, had heard from him in several days. I became really worried. I drove over to talk to the apartment manager. Since my name, not Rob's, was on the lease, the manager agreed that we could go check on Rob together. As we opened the apartment door and looked inside, both of us stood in abject horror. Not only did the place smell like a garbage bin, but every square inch of wall space was spray-painted. Rob had sprayed words of profanity everywhere, including on the ceiling. I'm talking about every curse word you can imagine. The place was completely destroyed.

Well, naturally, the apartment manager freaked out and called the police. I couldn't locate Rob for the next several days. When he finally showed back up at the apartment, the manager called me, and I came over. Rob never did tell me where he'd been, but I suspected he had been with Trent. I asked, "Rob, what happened to your apartment? The entire place is destroyed."

"What? You're kidding. Someone must have broken in."

Um, yeah, right. "Rob, you have no belongings," I said. "The entire place looks like a scene out of a horror movie. The ceiling fan is on the floor, and the refrigerator has been disassembled. People don't break in and do that."

Because it was my John Hancock on the lease, I was left holding the bag and had to pay for all the damages. They were major: holes in the wall, appliances disassembled, walls spray-painted with vile words. There was hardly an inch of space that Rob hadn't destroyed in his drug-induced rage.

Finally, he admitted he had been doing drugs . . . a lot of drugs. Honestly, I think he was too wasted to comprehend anything past that. I had no choice at this point. I knew I had to get him help. My first call was to Cedars-Sinai, a massive nonprofit medical center, but they didn't have a drug-treatment program. If Rob wasn't willing to be admitted to a treatment center once he was discharged, they couldn't force him.

I confronted Rob about his drug use and told him he had to get help. Not surprisingly, he changed his story. "I don't have a drug problem!" he barked. "Okay, so maybe I do drugs sometimes, but I can stop anytime I want."

Yeah, so says the addict.

I knew I had to figure out how to get him into that treatment program, with or without his willingness. This had become a matter of life and death, and I knew it. I learned that people are either admitted voluntarily, or they can be compelled by the courts if they break the law. *Hmmm*, I thought, *the court system.*

That's where I got my break. I hatched an elaborate scheme. I mean, this was brilliant. Okay, it wasn't elaborate or brilliant, but I was kind of proud of myself for having come up with it, nonetheless.

I first went to the West Hollywood Police. "I need to speak to a detective, please," I said.

"Yes, sir," the cop behind the bulletproof glass said. "What is this regarding?"

I looked behind me at the other people seated in the waiting area. "Uh, it's confidential."

"One moment," he replied.

I couldn't believe it, but not ten minutes later, a detective emerged and took me back to his tiny office. We'll call him "Detective Steve."

"How can I help you?" he said.

These cops were friendly. I don't know why it struck me so hard, but it did. "I've got a problem," I said, "a life-and-death problem. If I don't do something right now, someone very dear to me is going to die." Detective Steve listened intently as I continued, "I have a friend named Rob. Rob has become strung out on drugs. He's gotten himself into male prostitution. At the rate he's going, I am not sure he'll be alive in a month unless I can get him into an involuntary drug-rehab program."

To this day, I'm still amazed at the response I got. When I went in there, I figured this would be a complete waste of time, but as I explained the situation further, this detective was actually willing to help me. I don't know, he must have lost someone close to him to drugs at some point in his life, because he and I came up with a plan.

The next day, our plan went into motion. I called Detective Steve and he said they were ready, so I went in to talk to Rob. "Look," I said, "you keep asking to borrow my car, and I keep saying no. I feel like an asshole. So, here." I held out my car keys.

It was early in the day, but Rob was already wasted. "I knew you loved me," he replied as he snatched the keys out of my hand. He was up and out the door without saying goodbye. I heard the engine start, and I slumped into the couch. It was a setup. Rob didn't get two blocks down the road before he found blue lights in his rearview mirror.

He pulled the car over to the curb, and when the officer approached, apparently Rob laid it on pretty thick. He cried and bawled as he pleaded with the officer to let him go. However, the West Hollywood Police are pretty good at dealing with drama queens. The cop performed a sobriety test on Rob, and of course, Rob failed it on an epic scale.

When I spoke to the patrol officer later, the first thing he said was, "Your friend was so wasted, there was no question I was going to arrest him. From there, he was forcibly drug-tested." Once Rob failed the drug test, he was admitted to Cedars-Sinai.

It was the first time I would pay for Rob's rehab, and it cost me $40,000.

Falling Apart

Los Angeles has perhaps the worst traffic in the world, and trekking over to Cedars-Sinai from Orange County, California, was killing me. Rob finally agreed to enter a drug-treatment center, and I had him transferred to UCLA Medical Center. Since he was forcibly detained there, he couldn't just leave, which was a relief for me. However, with all of the drama of this situation, my job performance began to suffer. I wasn't getting any sleep, I wasn't keeping up with my clients as well as I should have, and I was letting my side business selling white-label cosmetics fall apart.

Emotionally, I was drained. Rob broke down crying every time I visited, which was almost daily. He'd fall to the ground, grab me by the leg, and not let go. "Please, please don't leave me!" he'd say.

I would have to drag him across the floor until he finally released his hold. It was mind-numbing. Speaking of mind-numbing, the doctors at UCLA said Rob had done so many drugs that he was heading to the threshold of brain damage.

Several weeks later, Rob turned the corner. He genuinely seemed to want to stay clean. He was released from the treatment program. As I prepared for his homecoming, one thing I realized was that he shouldn't be around the same environment he was before. It would be too tempting for him to slip right back into the drug scene. So, I got us an apartment in Los Feliz, a relaxed hillside neighborhood of Los Angeles that draws a bunch of creative types. It's a pretty cool area.

Rob swore he was off drugs for good. What a load of crap that turned out to be. Within a week, he was strung out again and was rearrested. That one cost me $3,000 in bench warrants. I mean, I was bailing him out, but I was near the breaking point.

One day, we were in my car and we started arguing. At a stoplight, Rob jumped out and ran away. I cried pretty hard that day and said to myself, "I'm losing it. I have to get out of this." But, as you might have guessed, I wasn't strong enough to break free.

In the meantime, Rob's family back home in New Jersey had no idea just how bad his behavior and drug abuse had become. Rob had been lying to them all along. As far as his mother knew, Rob "worked in LA at a beauty company owned by this Vince Spinnato guy." Rob certainly was never employed by me. Little did his mother know, Rob was a drugged-out male prostitute.

As it turns out, Rob's uncle on his mother's side was gay, and out of the blue, the guy called me one night. I don't know, I guess he figured that since he and I were both gay, we could talk freely. He had apparently gotten a bad feeling about Rob's evasiveness with his mother, and he wanted to find out if anything was going on. So, I unloaded on him. I told him the whole story. He ended up relaying the information back to Rob's mom, and she, of course, started to lose her shit. I mean, she freaked right the hell out. I didn't know it at the time, but she had already lost her first two sons to drugs, and her daughter was in and out of jail for the same reason, so she was coming unglued.

The problem was, she blamed me for everything. From her point of view, this Vince guy was the problem. One day, she called me. "Why are you making my boy do drugs?" she yelled.

Wow, what a nutjob. I was so angry at her. "I'm not making him do anything, lady! I don't do drugs. Your son does drugs. Now, are you going to be part of the problem, or part of the solution?"

The mom decided to do nothing. I couldn't believe it, but in her defense, she had suffered so much by losing two other children to drugs that I guess she was in serious denial. Now that she and I were in touch, I was asking her for help, and she was giving me jack shit.

About two months went by as I spiraled further down the Rob-obsessed path. Then, Rob's lover, Trent, came back, and my world really started falling apart. I became incredibly suspicious of what Rob was doing with this guy. Rob continued to tell me they were just friends, but I didn't believe it. Eventually, I caught Rob and Trent together in a "compromising position," if you know what I mean. A confrontation erupted. I knew I was not in my right mind, but I was just so angry, so hurt. Rob, as you can imagine, was blasted out of his mind on drugs. I went home and cried for an hour. This time, I picked up the phone again. I called Rob's uncle and told him how bad it was, and that if something wasn't done quickly, Rob wouldn't be with us much longer. That finally lit a fire under Rob's mom's ass.

A couple of days later, I drove out to LAX to pick her up at the airport. We had never met face to face. We talked in the car, and it was awkward, to say the least. This woman didn't trust me at all. After a while, though, I could tell she was beginning to relax. Perhaps she realized that the Vince Spinnato guy, the guy she had blamed for all her son's problems, wasn't the problem, after all. However, I don't think she fully embraced that fact until she laid eyes on Rob. Here he was, her own son, and she could barely recognize him. He was gaunt, pale, and stoned out of his gourd. If you saw him today, you'd say he looked like a zombie.

As for Rob, I could tell he was shocked to see his mom. When he realized there was no way to hide what he had become—a drug addict—he accepted the situation. He hugged her and cried. She had come to LA with the express purpose of finding out what was going on with her son, and if necessary, taking him home with her. Unfortunately, she wasn't able to just snatch him up and put him on a plane bound for New Jersey the next morning. Rob was too wasted for that. So, she stayed for three days just trying to sober him up enough to fly. After all, she didn't want him to be arrested at the airport.

The morning they left, I waved goodbye to Rob as he and his mother boarded the plane. I swear, I didn't think I'd breathe again. It was the most painful time of my life.

Unfortunately, the whirlwind wasn't over yet.

SOMETHING IS WRONG

With Rob back in New Jersey and me in LA, I got some much-needed space. I began to focus on my career even harder, and also finally took a look at my finances. Oh, the shit had hit the fan. Upon tallying up what I had spent on Rob's damaged apartment, his various stints in drug-rehab centers, and everything else, I was shocked. I had dropped over $100,000 trying to get him clean. Although I was making fair money at the time, let me tell you, $100,000 puts a dent in your wallet!

I talked a good bit on the phone with Rob's uncle about what was going on in New Jersey. Rob's parents had enrolled him in a forty-day program in a rehab clinic. Yet, all the while, Rob was calling me, begging me to come to Jersey and get him out. Well, I may have been obsessed, but I wasn't stupid. Those phone calls were really emotional for me, though. Rob was so upset, and I was so in love with him that it nearly killed me to not help him. After we'd hang up, I'd cry for hours. *Am I doing the right thing?* I'd think to myself. It was maddening.

I distracted myself by taking a good look at the enormity of what I had spent on Rob. After all, my phone had started ringing off the hook from bill collectors. *Holy. Mother. Of. God.* Not only had I spent all that money on Rob; he had apparently been passing off bad checks—*my* bad checks. He had racked up another $100,000 in spending. I had no idea. When I found that out, my mouth dropped open. I was, probably for the first time in my life, speechless. The realizations only kept pouring in.

If Rob was passing off bad checks under my name, then I'm the one who was funding his drug habit. The truth hurt. It hurt badly.

In the years that have passed since that time, I finally have been able to forgive myself. Rob was particularly good at one thing: manipulation. He could manipulate people. He was a gifted liar, and he would go to any length to pull off his charades. He had manipulated me, and back home in New Jersey, he was finally able to manipulate his parents. About ten days into his forty-day treatment plan in New Jersey, Rob convinced his mom to get him out.

When I found out he had been released from rehab, I slumped onto the floor in my apartment and curled up into a ball. The lost love, the debt, the humiliation, the bill collectors . . . I was an emotional train wreck. I knew from personal experience just how bad of an idea releasing Rob was, but Rob's mom had rented him an apartment in northern New Jersey, and his antics started again.

I think you can pretty much predict how the Rob story ends. Only a couple of weeks later, about three months after his mom had taken him back to New Jersey, Valentine's Day came and went without me hearing from him. Concerned, I called his uncle. "Listen, something's wrong," I said. "I haven't heard from Rob, and he's not answering his phone. I'm worried."

In turn, the uncle called Rob's mom, and she drove out to his apartment to check on him. What she found was something no mother should ever encounter. Rob was dead. He had apparently been dead for three days, and a terrible stench was emanating from his apartment.

As overwhelming as that revelation was, and as sad as I was about it, there was also this tiny voice in the back of my head telling me that Rob had never been good for me. I may have loved him, but in his passing, somehow there was a sense of relief. I've never been able to tell anyone that, but all these years later, I can.

Rob's passing marked a new dawn for me. Today, I look back over all the things that transpired, and I shake my head. While I'm amazed and even appalled at some of my actions then, I sort of understand them. Thank God I grew out of them. Now, I channel my obsessions into my beauty business, and there, the obsessions thrive.

Nevertheless, I wanted to go to Rob's funeral. I knew it would be an important marker for me, an event that would signify the passing of an era in my life. In short, I needed closure. Yet, when I called Rob's uncle, he wasn't very forthcoming with the information. "Vince, listen . . . ah . . . there's something I need to tell you."

"What?" I replied.

"Rob's family, well, they feel . . ." He was trying to break the news to me gently. "They want this to be a family event."

"You mean they don't want me there?" I was mortified. I had done nothing but try to show love for Rob. I was the only one who had cared enough to be there, who had cared enough to try to save him. His family didn't do that; *I* did that.

"I'm sorry," was all he could say.

I'm not someone who wants to disrupt a family in their time of grief. However, this was my time of grief, too. Although I had no intention of bursting into the church service, I got on a plane and headed for New Jersey. When I landed, I made a few calls and was able to find out where the burial was to be held. I rented a car and drove out there.

The cemetery was a beautiful place: slightly rolling hills, well-kept grass, finely appointed pathways, and huge trees everywhere. It was peaceful. I kept my distance so no one would see me, and watched from afar as the family gathered around the gravesite. As they lowered Rob into the ground, I stood under a sprawling oak tree, alone, and wept.

Mr. Potato Head

After Rob's passing, my emotions were still in a whirlwind. Nonetheless, I was bound and determined to set my feet firmly on the ground and move forward with my life and career.

Shortly after Rob's funeral, I was recruited as an independent contractor at the strangest work environment of my career: a company we'll call "Silver Palace." I was brought on as leader of its beauty division. That's right, leader of the whole division. This time, I was in charge. This new role would later prove to be a phenomenal learning experience for me.

This new job as head of the beauty division resulted in a pretty damn good income for me, and I began to make a dent in the debt load I was carrying. It also gave me an opportunity to set money aside for something I'd desperately wanted since the time I was a big-nosed kid with a lisp: plastic surgery.

I decided to rent a house and move away from apartment living. I found this fabulous real estate agent (and by *fabulous*, I mean fabulously *gay*), and since I wasn't ready to plunk down a million dollars to buy a place just yet, he took me around to look at houses for lease. The one he helped me find was to die for, and it certainly wasn't just some ordinary place. We pulled into the driveway and I gasped. The place was not only aesthetically stunning, it was the home of a former star. This place was amazing. The views of LA were spectacular, and I was thrilled. I signed the lease on the spot.

But, back to business. Silver Palace had a line of beauty products, but they also manufactured and sold all-natural cereals, herbal teas, and a line of massage products sold mainly in Whole Foods. The company was totally owned by Sikhs. If you're not familiar with what that means, Sikhism is a monotheistic religion founded in India. These men and women are big believers in meditation, which, if you've never done it, is far cooler than you might imagine. They believe in things that are really pretty sensible: one God, equality of all humans, serving others, social justice, prosperity for all, honest conduct, yada yada yada. Interestingly, the owners of this big beauty firm, Silver Palace, were trying to conduct business in America using those beliefs. Quite the dichotomy to typical American business culture, you might say.

Prior to this time, I never knew what a Sikh was, nor what the followers practiced or believed. I just knew they dressed in all white, wore turbans on their heads, and never cut their hair or beards. Even though all of this was strange to me, they seemed like very nice people when I met with them. And, let's not forget that they offered me a higher salary than I had ever had. So, yeah, I was interested in the job.

While working at Silver Palace, someone wonderful came into my life. Her name was Laurel, and from the moment we met, I knew we would become friends. Laurel worked there as well, and our offices were right next to each other. In fact, the wall between us had a big sliding-glass window in it, and we kept it open all the time. We would cut up with each other, and I learned quickly that her laugh was infectious.

The company's corporate offices were actually in Eugene, Oregon, which, my God, is such a beautiful place. Although most of my time was spent in LA, I frequently traveled to Eugene. Since I had been in a lot of labs that formulated beauty products, I had a lot of experience with how the finished formulations were later produced. That experience paid off when the company asked me to help them improve and modernize their manufacturing facility.

It was time to shift Silver Palace's thinking away from tea and cereal to ramp up their existing beauty business. This was a great opportunity for me. I mean, I was actually helping them decide on how they should set up their manufacturing process. Millions of dollars were spent based on my direction. This time, *I* was the expert. *I* was the one calling the shots. Vinny was in charge! My job involved educating Silver Palace on the process of formulation and manufacturing, and since they wanted to get into private-label cosmetics, I focused on that. You can imagine how exciting this was for me.

I really wish I could take you back there with me, because it was the type of place you have to experience for yourself. Everything about this workplace was different: the culture, the way people dressed, their demeanor, and even their names. Since this was an Indian culture, everyone's names were incredibly different from ours. I'm not just talking about the Indian people there. Once you become a Sikh, even if you were born in Topeka, Kansas, to a couple of white people, you get an Indian name.

Although I did not want to become a Sikh myself, this was all fascinating to me. However, one of the things I wasn't too fond of was the fact that everyone was so serious. That's just not me. I go around lightly making fun of everything and everyone. I mean, life's too short to be miserable. You have no idea how deeply the culture was ingrained into the office environment. They even had inspirational mantras piped throughout the office. I'm talking twenty-four hours a day. If there wasn't an inspirational voice coming over the speaker, it was Indian music. You were *immersed*.

One day while I was trying to adjust to the music, Laurel walked by. I was sitting at my desk with a big, silly grin on my face, typing away and *singing* to the tune of the Indian music. I'm singing, "Bonnie blue, bonnie blue, bonnie-bonnie-bonnie blue," because I didn't have the foggiest idea what the lyrics really were. She stopped at my office door and peered in at me. We hardly knew each other at the time, but my eyes met hers and I just kept right on singing. Her face was stiff for just a second, then she cracked up. Before long, she was laughing so hard, she had to cover her mouth. We were fast friends after that.

As strange as the culture was, over time, I did start to admire the Sikhs and what they were about. Almost everybody who joined the organization ended up rolling into the Sikh thing, and they wanted me to as well. Although I did not convert, working there did mark the first time I tried yoga, which was really cool. Then came meditation, which helped me calm down just a bit. Believe me, back then, I needed some calming down.

The head of the organization was a man everyone simply called

"Guru." He was around seventy years old, and if you can believe this, he was a New York Jew in Sikh clothing. I'm not joking. This guy was a born-and-bred New Yorker, yet he had completely adopted the Sikh culture. He had a long gray beard, wore a turban and tunic-robe thing, and yet spoke with a Brooklyn accent! The accent killed me. The first time I met him, it was all I could do to hold it together.

Guru ended up taking me under his wing. He was a really smart guy, very grounded, and for an older man, he was in incredible physical shape. Eventually, Guru became a father figure to me, but he was so serious all the time that it bothered me. In fact, when I asked Laurel about it, she told me, "I haven't seen him laugh in the ten years I've been here."

I shook my head and said to her, "Laurel, I've got to do something about this." Insert devious, cackling Vinny laugh here. I mean, I was here for business, but dammit, we were going to have some fun, too. So, I changed the music that filtered through the office, I joked and cut up with everybody, and I generally tried to lighten the place up. I instituted "dance night" and convinced everyone to join in. I'd host it after hours in the office. I would get the music going and have people on the dance floor (and by *dance floor*, I mean we were rocking out in the kitchen). Slowly, people began to smile and laugh more in the office.

The longer I was with the company, the happier and freer people became. My colleagues called me "the cruise director of the promenade deck," because I had started pulling everyone together to go to lunch. To get these lunches organized, I would call our receptionist and say, "Gather the passengers. This cruise ship is about to make port. We're going to lunch!" These lunches were a great time.

Later in my time there, I had ten or fifteen Sikhs take me aside and tell me how much I had changed the company culture and how much I had changed Guru. He had been so stiff and staunch when I arrived, yet he was lightening up. Some days, there was even a smile!

Ultimately, we were really dedicated to producing a first-rate line of beauty products. Every single morning, we had a 7:45 a.m. conference call. Everyone else participated in the call on their way into work, but I lived way the hell over in Hollywood. It was a long drive, and my cell phone would cut out. So, I had to get to the office at the crack of dawn to participate in this phone call. It was nuts, but I was dedicated and not going to miss a single opportunity.

The further this job rolled forward, the more "green" rolled in. I was pulling in big corporate deals, where we were hired to produce lines of private-labeled beauty products for clients. We're talking about brands like Trader Joe's, Cost Plus World Market, and TJ Maxx. I was also putting together a megadeal with Kmart, which had the potential to be the biggest deal ever for me. Plus, I was making my mark in the beauty world and making a boatload of money in the process.

On top of paying down my personal debt, I started talking to Laurel about what I really wanted to do. This time, I wasn't talking about my desire to start my own brand. No, no, I was talking about plastic surgery, something I had wanted from the time the character on *Dynasty* had an accident and doctors changed his appearance. In the past, I had been so busy trying to buy Rob's love and selling white-label products, I had pushed the idea aside. When I finally made up my mind to take the plunge, I pulled Laurel over to my office.

"Why are you acting so weird?" she said with a giggle.

I whispered, "I've been saving money for plastic surgery since I started working here."

"Plastic . . . what are you talking about? You don't exactly need a tummy tuck."

"No, dummy," I teased. "I want to do my nose and some other stuff with my face." After all, this was California. Everyone had had one thing or another done to themselves.

Laurel got behind me 100 percent. She was just that kind of girl, and I loved her for it. She was there for me through anything. You've got to understand, Laurel and I were just nuts. We did all kinds of things to entertain ourselves. Now that I'd revealed my secret to her, what did Laurel do? The next morning, she showed up at my office door with her hands behind her back. She began to laugh.

"What is so funny, you lunatic?" I asked. She pulled her hands out from behind her back to reveal a Mr. Potato Head doll. I laughed and said, "Okay, what's that for?"

She yanked all the parts off of his face and said, "Each time you have a surgery, we'll put that part onto him until they're all there!" She thought that was the funniest thing in the world. So, that's what we did.

The first surgery was rhinoplasty (a nose job), and then otoplasty (surgery to have my ears pinned back). Before you could say the words, Laurel put a nose and ears on Mr. Potato Head. It became our little secret.

In line with my life not always working out well, the nose job was a failure and had to be revised. Then, I added a brow lift before going under again for liposuction to flatten my tummy. Not long after, I began getting implants, beginning with my chin, cheeks, and jaw. Never satisfied, I followed that with abdominal etching—a nine-hour surgery—followed by pectoral implants. My rationale: no matter how many hours I spent at the gym lifting weights, my abs and pecs never changed. That's around the time a doctor diagnosed me with body dysmorphia. I was so obsessed with changing perceived faults in my appearance, things no one else saw.

But did I stop there? Nooo. I couldn't even if I had wanted to. Why?

Well, my body always seemed to be working against me. The pecs rejected and had to be removed. The result was my first methicillin-resistant Staphylococcus-aureus diagnosis, commonly known as MRSA. It's a severe life-threatening infection with only limited treatment. It was a long recovery, and fortunately, Guru was sympathetic.

Did I learn from all this pain and suffering? Not Vinny. I had a hole in my soul the size of the Grand Canyon because of my appearance. So, back to the cutting table I went.

I had another tummy tuck, then tried pec implants a second time. They rejected again, requiring yet another painful surgery to remove them. In fact, no matter how many surgeries I had, my body either rejected the procedure or my appearance didn't change. Friends joked that the doctors put me to sleep, smacked me around a bit, then sewed me back up.

To me, it's no joke. My entire life, I have been pursuing beauty—for myself and for others by founding my own cosmetic firm. What I failed to see was that internal beauty is far more important, a fact I wouldn't come to fully understand for more than another decade when I visited Auschwitz, the epicenter of German evil during WWII. But, that's a story for later.

All in all, I've had around thirty surgeries over the years. Most were during my stint with Silver Palace. Somehow, in between them, I kept bringing in clients and working on enormous corporate deals. Sears, Marshalls, and Kmart were in play, and I was courting them. Each had their sights set on rolling out their own private-label beauty products, and it was Vinny to the rescue. I traveled all over the place pitching our capabilities, and the corporate decision-makers loved the profits . . . with a few reservations.

All of this was new to the company. Guru and the other leaders were still struggling to make the transition from cereal and tea to beauty products, even though that's what they had hired me to do in the first place. The more deals I brought in, the more I believed I was convincing them to stay the course. After all, these private-label deals have long sales cycles. It might take eighteen months to close a deal of that size, but I encouraged Guru to be patient.

Meanwhile, the Sikhs weren't done trying to convince me to follow their practices. They'd have loved me to grow a beard and don a turban. Since I had embraced meditation, they felt they were making progress with me. That's when they sent me out to commemorate the winter solstice, and it was one weird-ass gathering. It wasn't a festival exactly, but more of a community event that happened north of Santa Fe. Guru led the entire thing . . . and when I say he led it, I mean he was the man in charge. Before you think this was just one of those corporate team-building events that we all hate, this thing was massive. Mega-freaking-apocalyptic massive, with tens of thousands of participants.

We practiced meditation, yoga, and chanting, and heard lectures on self-reliance, radical inclusion, self-expression, and acts of giving. We went on long barefoot "healing walks," which, by the way, I hated. I never understood why someone would want to be barefoot.

After all, how can a person sport their $1,100 fur-lined Louis Vuitton slippers if they are barefoot?

The whole thing was very new age and earthy. After a few days of tromping around in the dirt, everyone was filthy, but nobody really seemed to care. Well, except me, that is. I couldn't help but wonder the entire time, *My God, is there no shower here?* As I've said, I'm a total neat freak. In fact, having my body or home get dirty is one of my phobias. So, I did what any neatnik would do: I tried to cleanse my body with baby wipes. Everyone thought it was so hilarious, they took a picture of me.

On the drive back to LA, Guru asked me in his best Brooklyn accent, "So, what did you think?" He really wanted the experience to have transformed me into the Sikh way of being.

I didn't know how to break it to him, but I couldn't lie to the man, either. I said, "Can we talk about the Kmart deal I'm trying to put together?"

I think that was all it took. He knew I would never be a Sikh.

A Darlin' Offer

When I got back from the desert, I took ample time to scrub the dirt from my toes, head, fingernails, eyelids, and behind my ears. Then, I came back into the office, but before I got back to work, I told Laurel about a guy I had met online. She got very excited about the possibilities because, like I said before, she was a very positive person. She saw the best in everyone, and I think that trait rubbed off on me.

His name was Noah, and he lived in LA. Of course, after the crushing loss of Rob, my sensibilities were more than a bit off kilter, and I second-guessed everything. I was confused, but sweet Laurel would listen to me intently. She convinced me to continue going out with this new guy.

I was a happy puppy. To give you the quick background, this was one cute dude. After meeting online, we chatted back and forth online for about three or four days, then got on the phone. We were attracted to each other from the get-go. Noah was three and a half years into an undergraduate degree, was very independent, took damn good care of himself, had a job with a design agency, and paid his own bills. In other words, he was a total departure from my previous boyfriends.

We hit it off right away, although I've got to say, he was more attracted to me than I was to him at first. Noah was about six-foot-three, which I found very overwhelming. I remember telling Laurel about our first real date. I told her that I had a really nice time, but I was kind of vain about it. She could tell by my description that Noah wasn't what I was used to attraction-wise. But, Laurel being Laurel, she encouraged me to go out with him again.

For our second date, Noah and I went to an upscale shopping center, restaurant, and club scene. Noah was younger and still into staying out at a nightclub drinking and dancing, but I really wasn't into it. Noah told me, "If you want to go home now, no problem. Just grab my keys from the valet and go home. We can talk tomorrow."

It was very considerate of him. *Great*, I thought. *I've finally met someone who doesn't just think of himself.* I walked outside and handed the valet the ticket, and he ran around the side and came back with Noah's black Volkswagen Jetta. When I got in the car, I remember thinking, *What the hell are these baby booties doing in here?* I brushed if off, then drove home and fell asleep, exhausted.

It wasn't ten minutes later that the phone started to ring. I let it go to voicemail a couple of times before I finally got up to answer the third call. "Who the hell is calling me so late?" I said into the phone.

"Sir!" a young man exclaimed. "This is the valet. You've got the wrong car!" Sure as shit, I had taken someone else's black Volkswagen. From then on, I vowed to pay more attention to detail so I wouldn't get caught up in these debacles. The first thing I did was start putting a lot of effort into my relationship with Noah. Even though the timing wasn't good for a new relationship, seeing as my travel schedule was ramping up and I was moving forward on several business deals, I was ready for one.

Career-wise, despite filling the sales pipeline at Silver Palace with one potential private-label deal after another, I was always looking for more. One of my next business trips took me back to Florida. Now, I know what you are thinking. *Vinny is going to go to another hotel pool and get himself stuck in another tube slide.* Well, I had no intention of repeating that little incident. This trip was for yet another trade show. I went onto the show floor and pressed palms, as one does. Later that day, I was hanging out by the hotel pool and sitting by myself on a chair. I had my shades on, a set of fabulous designer bathing trunks, and I was lathered with suntan lotion. I took one glance at the tube slides and muttered, "You couldn't *pay* me to go down that thing."

"What was that?" a voice beside me answered.

I turned. "Oh, sorry. Talking to myself, I guess."

The guy was lying out in the sun and trying to relax a bit, just like anyone else, and we got to talking. It was small talk at first, but he started asking me a lot about my work. Once he found out what I did for a living, the questions came rapid-fire. After several minutes of this barrage of questions, I felt like I was monopolizing the conversation. As I went to ask him something about himself, he fired another beauty-product question at me. Damn, this guy was intense! Finally, he introduced himself. I won't use his real name here, but when he said it, I paused. *It can't be,* I thought to myself. "Wait a minute," I said. "Aren't you the CEO of Coppertone?"

Just as sure as Dolly Parton must sleep on her back, this guy was their chief executive officer at the parent organization, formerly owned by Merck & Co., one of the largest companies on the planet. I couldn't believe it! I mean, what are the odds that I'd be shooting the shit with a guy at the pool, and he turns out to have more money than God?

I tried to contain myself, but I wasn't going to let the opportunity pass me by. He started talking to me about the brand. At the time, they were looking for somebody to take the sunscreen brand to the next level. Since he kept talking, I kept nodding my head. It wasn't much later when he turned to me and said, "Hey, some business associates and I are taking a yacht out tomorrow morning. Why don't you come along?"

The CEO of Coppertone had just invited me on a yacht outing with him. I knew good and well that this was a preliminary job interview. So, you can bet that the next morning I was on that dock. The yacht was gorgeous. We set sail, and it was first class all the way. It had a captain, a couple of crew members, and even a couple of stewards serving food and drinks. I was positively giddy to be there.

As it turns out, the role he was trying to fill at Coppertone wasn't really a good fit for me. Although I would have looked fabulous on a Coppertone billboard at Waikiki Beach, the reality was, I was more of a specialist in private-label beauty, and they were looking for a brand guy. Anyway, one of the guests on the boat happened to work for a company that was a little more up my alley. In fact, she worked in the corporate offices of Estée Lauder in Manhattan.

Estée-fricking-Lauder! I had tried to get into that place a dozen times, but that was back before I had all this experience. At the time, they owned twenty-nine beauty brands, including Clinique, Aveda, Origins, Prescriptives, Aramis, and Bobbi Brown. Just being next to her was almost enough to give me palpitations.

She and I got to talking, and it wasn't long before she began to tell me about a job they were trying to fill. "Dahling," she said, "would you be at all interested in interviewing for an executive role in product development? We need someone on the Clinique brand."

I almost flipped over the railing. This was huge! I mean, I was thriving at Silver Palace, but Estée, Clinique's parent company, is one of the biggest brands in the game. A job offer from Estée Lauder represented the chance of a lifetime. Obviously, I told her I was interested, and she and I made arrangements.

A few days later, I was back in LA. Let me tell you, to walk back into the Silver Palace offices after coming off a yacht, having just been courted by one of the biggest names in the beauty industry, was surreal, to say the least. Maybe it was the Indian music. Maybe it was the Sikh mantras filtering through the speakers. I don't know, but I knew it was time for a change.

I told Laurel all about what had happened. She was so excited and kept telling me I had to take the Estée Lauder job. With that in mind, the next thing I did may surprise you. I told my boss about it. That's right, I went in to see Guru and told him the whole story.

Now, I realize that telling your boss you just interviewed for a better job doesn't typically go over well. But, like I said, he and I were very close, and I wanted to share this with him. Again, he was like a father figure and was very supportive of me. While I'm not sure if Guru was surprised to find me interviewing for another job, he was well aware that I wanted to start my own beauty company one day. As we discussed this new job opportunity, he began asking me about my long-term ambitions.

"Vinny, I want you to do something for me," he said as we sat in his office. "I want you to close your eyes."

It was such a Sikh thing to say. I closed my eyes.

"Now, take a deep breath in through the nose, and hold it."

Another unbelievably Sikh-yoga-meditation-health-nut-California thing to say.

"Good, that's it. Now, exhale slowly through the mouth. Clear your mind. I want you to picture these two paths for your future life. One, a lucrative career in Manhattan, the other, the beginning of your own product line. Which path do you see yourself on?"

It took me no time at all to answer. "My own beauty line."

"Now, open your eyes."

He was like that. He could see things you couldn't see in yourself, like my yearning to have my own firm, and I loved him for it.

"My son, I don't want you to leave us," he said. "I don't want you to leave *me*. And after all, you've just admitted in front of God and myself that what you really want in your heart is to start your own line. I don't think that pursuing this role at Estée Lauder takes you down that path."

"But, I'd learn even more about how the big brands operate."

"On the contrary, dear boy."

"But—"

"Take a look at what you have here. Take a good look." His voice was soft, disarming. "You are on the cusp of closing the best deal the company has ever made. You've worked on it for eighteen months, and you are *so* close. You know I want nothing more than for you to succeed. So, here is what I am offering you."

I was taken aback. It never occurred to me that he might make a counteroffer to Estée Lauder. I slid forward in my chair.

He continued, "I am increasing your annual salary to three hundred fifty thousand dollars."

Did he just triple my salary?

"I want you to close the Kmart deal. It's a one-point-five-million-dollar commission straight into your pocket." Then, he said something I'll never forget. "After that, I want to personally back you as you go out and start your own private-label business."

I nearly died. "Wait, you want to do *what?*" I stuttered.

He smiled and stood from behind his desk. He walked over to me, put a hand on my shoulder, and looked me in the eye. "The Estée Lauder offer is a wonderful recognition of how hard you've worked and the skills you possess. But, your destiny lies on a different path." He walked out of his office.

I sat there in stunned silence. "Holy shit, Batman," I said. Just as sure as Robin is gay, that man had just offered to finance me. I was mystified and really confused. How could I turn down the Estée Lauder job offer? I knew it was the job of a lifetime, but the entrepreneur's voice in me would not shut up. I knew deep down in my heart that I wanted to launch my own business, and Guru had just offered to finance me.

Over the next two days, Guru cemented his earlier statements. He put my new salary and commission structure in writing. Plus, he added a nice little caveat into the contract: a severance package. If I lost my job or was fired for any reason, they had to pay me severance.

Meanwhile, Estée Lauder kept calling me. It was time to make a decision.

This was really hard for me, and I lost a lot of sleep over it. During this time, my relationship with Noah was growing, and he was a part of my decision process. After all, if I accepted the job in New York, I'd be leaving him behind. Since I was becoming more attached to him, that was something I had trouble picturing.

So, between being assured that I was going to be supported and financed by Silver Palace, the impending $1.5 million commission I stood to earn, and my blossoming romance with Noah, I turned the Estée Lauder position down.

Laurel was happy for me and disappointed at the same time. As much as she wanted me to stay at Silver Palace, she felt the Estée Lauder position would have been perfect for me. However, she understood where I was coming from. She understood my relationship with Noah was becoming more serious. She also understood my desire to obtain financing to start my own line. Even so, she said something that haunts my thoughts to this day: "It's just that, well, I think Guru needs to put the offer to finance you in writing."

Not listening to her turned out to be one of the biggest mistakes of my life.

My Elvis Moment

Like I said, my relationship with Noah was progressing. You might even say it had taken hold . . . hard. Noah lived in Anaheim, California, at the time, and he was really into "stuff," meaning he liked cars, clothes, and electronics. Whatever it was, if it was fancy and had a lot of bling going on, he was in. Maybe that was what attracted him to me in the first place. I was a guy who liked stuff, too. I lived in a swanky house with a great view, I dressed in designer clothes at all times, and I had two Mercedes.

Yeah, I know, one guy with two Mercedes. It doesn't make sense, but that was me. It wasn't until years later and a massive amount of therapy that I realized how much importance I'd placed on physical beauty and fancy things, all of which I thought said to the world, "Vinny is one effing successful guy!"

So, yes, Noah was a really nice guy, but the more time we spent together, the more he saw that I was capable of spending an awful lot of money on him. He began acting irresponsibly regarding work: coming in late, not showing up, etc. It didn't seem to bother him. He also slacked off on paying bills, then came to me for help. That was bad enough, but then I noticed a change in his attitude, and not for the better. He became snooty and condescending, making disparaging comments about the cars other people were driving. This was the beginning of an increase in arrogance with him.

About a month and a half later, Noah lost his job. I wasn't the least bit surprised. He called me from Anaheim crying. "Vinny, I've never lost a job before," he said.

"Well, no shit you lost your job. You're late for work every day!" Okay, so I didn't say that. In actuality, I consoled him, but I have often wondered whether he sabotaged his job in the first place. I always had the impression Noah thought I was living a life of leisure, that somehow money just came easily to me. Nothing was further from the truth. I busted my ass back then, and I still bust my ass today.

I drove down to Anaheim to comfort him. When I arrived, he was still very upset. I said, "Let's go to lunch. It will make you feel better." My grandiosity kicked in. At lunch I said, "Look, why don't I just give you what you were making per month? You can continue to live here, and you can keep going to school. After that, you can open your own design firm."

He seemed excited about the idea. Who wouldn't be? I had offered to pay him just to be alive. In retrospect, yeah, it was a dumb move on my part. But again, this was a long time ago, and I had yet to mature into the man I've become today. If I had been the person I am today, I would have instead poured that money into my own business.

At any rate, he had been upset and I felt like I was helping him. If you've followed the basic flow of my relationships up to this point, then you already know what I'm about to tell you. You see, based on what Noah saw of me financially—the house, the cars, the designer clothes—he had built up a very unrealistic idea of how much money I actually had. In retrospect, I don't blame him for coming to the wrong conclusion, but in reality, I didn't really have that kind of money. Instead, I had that kind of *debt*. The American dream, right?

He started making demands. "I want a car."

"A car?" I replied.

"A new car. Something high end."

Shit. You *know* what I did. I pulled "an Elvis." Elvis Presley had this habit of buying pink Cadillacs for the people in his life. Then again, he could afford it. I, on the other hand, just couldn't say no to Noah. I ended up helping him lease a Jaguar coupe. *Flick* went my credit card as I snapped it onto the car dealer's desk. I plunked down the cashola for the down payment, and he leased the rest. Wow, I was a chump back then. I literally didn't know how to say no to someone, particularly someone like Noah. He was able to manage the lease payment with the unemployment check he was receiving on top of the cash I was giving him. Unfortunately, after he drove it home, the spending wasn't done yet.

"Tinted windows," he blurted.

"Tinted—"

"I have to have tinted windows. Tinted windows are all the rage. They're the most awesome thing since God invented glass."

Flick went my credit card as I snapped it onto the desk at the window-tinting place.

Almost immediately, I started catching crap from some of my friends. "Vinny, what's going on?" they said. "You can't go around buying cars for people. This boyfriend of yours is taking advantage of you."

"No, you don't get it. It's not like that. He and I—"

"He's taking advantage," came the interrupted replies.

Dammit, I wish I had listened to them. They had my best interests at heart. I honestly didn't feel like I was buying Noah's affection or anything like that, and yet that's exactly what was happening. It was that same old pattern I'd had with Rob, and I should have realized it. Back then, I wasn't able to recognize these patterns like I am today. I also wasn't good at seeing things coming down the pike.

When Noah and I had our first Christmas together, he told me he loved me. That was the first time *anyone* had ever told me they loved me. I was elated, but otherwise, things were not good. He began to get drunk a lot. We would go to nice restaurants and he always drank, meaning a meal that should have cost fifty dollars ended up costing one hundred. *Flick* went the credit card onto the table. It was getting very expensive.

He would get drunk, behave badly, and pass out. I have no tolerance for people who act like that. Still, he was tender the rest of the time, and he would smooth things over.

He and I talked about living together, but neither of us was really ready. Even so, Noah did get involved in decorating my house. He ended up having the furniture custom made for me, because he knew a lot of vendors in the interior-design space and could get a huge discount. Since I wasn't ready for him to move in with me, I rented an apartment for him just ten minutes away from the house I had leased. The problem was, he wanted to move his friend Zoe into the apartment, too. Zoe was just his friend, but they were like two peas in a pod, always together. Almost everything had to be a package deal with Noah and Zoe, so he finally talked me into letting her move in, too.

When Noah moved up to LA, it did something to me. I don't know how to explain it. It was like a light switch going on inside my head. I suddenly began to realize what my friends were seeing, and it was the same crap they had seen in Rob. I paid for his car, his apartment, his salary, his little live-in friend. Hell, I paid for everything! Even though we were intimate with each other, it didn't help that he had told me he "wanted to take it slow."

"Slow?" I said. "What the fuck are you talking about? I just got you an apartment in LA so you could be closer to me!"

Ironically, once he moved to LA, I saw him even less. The situation almost mirrored what happened with Rob. History was repeating itself. Noah went to all the clubs in West Hollywood, and I started becoming jealous and worried. If I'm honest, I was getting pretty pissed off about it. In the meantime, I hosted a big party for his college graduation. I swear, I think I spent about ten grand on it. The party was going full swing, and he started getting drunk. Then, he got drunker.

What I saw next turned my stomach. During the party, I looked across the pool in my backyard. There was Noah. He was in the

Jacuzzi *making out with some girl.* Keep in mind, Noah was as gay as a hatbox full of Speedos, yet he was kissing a girl! Next, he went off and started kissing some guy I didn't even know. I had spent a fortune on this party for him, and here he was, acting like that. The whole thing was extremely embarrassing. He tried to make excuses, saying he was too drunk to know what he was doing, but I had a hard time stomaching that.

The truth was, he was afraid to lose me. In hindsight, his fear of losing me was more related to the fact that I was his meal ticket, so he couldn't just walk out. Well, I began pushing a lot. I wanted to spend more time with him, yet the more time we spent together, the more arguments we got into. Still, parts of the relationship felt really good, and I didn't want that to end.

As our one-year anniversary approached, I wanted to do something special. *Uh-oh,* you are probably thinking. *What did Vinny do this time? Buy him a Lamborghini?* No, but I did take him to Maui, Hawaii. We had a wonderful time swimming with the turtles, parasailing, eating great dinners. Everything felt like we were back on track.

Upon our return, Noah got a job at a retail store so he would have money for living expenses. I could tell, though, that he was starting to pull away from me. I responded in my usual way by trying to buy his love. Dammit!

Around that same time, I hadn't been feeling well, so I went to the doctor. Well, let me rephrase that. I felt like warmed-over vomit, so I went to the doctor. Yeah, that feels more like it. I'm not kidding you, though. I have never felt worse in my life.

My doctor looked at me and said, "No wonder you feel so bad. You've got pancreatitis."

"Pan-cre-a-what?"

Pancreatitis is an inflammation of the pancreas. Mild cases can go away on their own, but severe cases can be life-threatening. Normally, the pancreas produces stuff to help with digestion and hormones so your body can process sugar. However, when something goes wrong, the pancreas swells, and oh, my God, it hurts like hell.

The look on the doctor's face was one I'll never forget. He didn't bother replying. Instead, he picked up a phone in the exam room and dialed 911. Needless to say, this was no joke, and I was rushed to the hospital. My stomach had become totally distended, and to this day, it was the most painful thing I've ever been through. It felt like someone was constantly kicking me from the inside out and stepping on my organs. I was completely debilitated.

However, as physically painful as it was, it didn't hurt nearly as much as what happened next. As I recovered in the hospital bed after undergoing life-saving treatment, Noah didn't visit—not on day one, day two, or day three. I was so hurt. I couldn't believe it. I mean, Laurel, my close friend from Silver Palace, was there in a heartbeat. She was so wonderful to me. Yet, Noah didn't even bother to show up. He didn't come sit with me. He didn't call. He didn't do anything. It was horrible. It was on the fourth day that he wandered in with his tail between his legs. He had a little flower in his hand, a violet.

I was still so sick, I wasn't even able to sit up in bed. Tears welled in my eyes. I said, "It's been four days, Noah."

"Well, I knew you weren't feeling well, and I didn't want to bother you."

When I finally got back home, I found a long letter from him sitting on the kitchen counter. Before picking it up, I just sat and stared at the envelope for a while. I knew what it would say. It was a breakup letter. Noah had not only moved out of the apartment I'd rented for him, he had broken up with me.

I felt like I had been gut-punched again.

Nevertheless, I had to hold it together. I needed to go to work every day, and I needed to stay focused on my professional life. All too soon, Laurel's warning about Guru putting his offer to finance me in writing would come back to haunt me.

Kmart or Bust

I had turned down Estée Lauder two months prior to getting sick, and despite not being quite up to par physically, I was pressing forward on the Kmart deal. I was determined to not let up on that deal until it closed.

One day, Guru walked into my office. "Vinny, we have to talk," he said. "I have some news."

If you know me, you'll know I'm barely able to speak without trying to crack a joke. So, I smiled and said, "What is it? Are you finally coming out of the closet?"

He didn't think that was funny. In fact, his back stiffened. What he said next sucked the air right out of my lungs. "We've given it a lot of thought. I'm sorry. We're moving back to our core business. We're shutting down the beauty division."

Well. Screw. Me. Sideways. I was stunned.

He wasn't done. "We've spent a lot of money on your division, and it hasn't paid off. We're going to stick with what we know."

"But . . . we're this close," I said, holding my thumb and forefinger about an inch apart. "The Kmart deal is so close, I can almost taste the Blue Light Special! Jesus Christ, Guru, they've got twenty-one hundred stores. It's a twenty-five-million-dollar deal."

"You keep working on that, Vinny," he replied in his Brooklyn-Sikh accent. "We may be shutting down your division, but we want that deal."

He didn't want a beauty division, but the prospect of a $25 million deal was too much to pass up. Needless to say, I sat in stunned silence. Although I couldn't see my own face at the time, I'm pretty sure I scowled, and I hate scowling; it wrinkles the skin.

All I could do was move on. Over the next several weeks, I continued pressing forward with Kmart. I knew that closing that deal might be my last act as an employee of Silver Palace, but I wanted that commission so badly. You've got to understand how much goes into a deal of that size. These things take a long time to come to fruition. It can easily take eighteen months from start to finish. Yet, Guru just didn't get it. Forty-five more days went by, and the deal still wasn't closed.

"Vinny," he said as he walked into my office, "how come the Kmart thing is still hanging out there?"

"Because the people at Kmart are not idiots," I replied. I could tell by the look on his face that that hadn't gone over well. "Guru, I've told you. A deal of this size requires patience. Kmart isn't playing games. They're a serious company with serious money, and they are making damn sure they're about to spend it with the right partner. I'm making sure of that. *That's* why you hired me."

"This isn't working. I'm sorry, Vinny. You are fired."

My mouth dropped open. "Are you kidding me?"

Nothing, absolutely nothing could have prepared me for that moment. It was the worst betrayal of my life. He walked out. After a moment of just sitting there stunned, I thought, *That's it? It's over? My career at Silver Palace, my daily laugh sessions with Laurel, and my Kmart deal?* Then, I sat bolt-upright in my chair. *My Kmart deal? Wait a damned minute. There's no way I'm going to let that fall apart!*

I ran after him. "What about your promise to fund my own cosmetic line?"

He didn't answer.

My family, friends, Laurel—*everybody* was shocked that Silver Palace had shit-canned their entire beauty division. There was one thing I decided right then and there: I was not going to crumble into a mass of blubbering crap over being fired. I was going to figure out how to get that damned Kmart deal without them.

First, I went after the severance package that I had, thankfully, gotten in writing. Guru balked at the idea of paying it, but I wasn't taking any shit. I wasn't going to let him take further advantage of me. This was business, and I intended to get exactly what I had been promised. The severance package was about $80,000, and I made sure they gave me every penny. They tried to guilt-trip me about it, but I insisted. The moral of the story here is that in business, Vinny will do exactly what he is supposed to do, and more. It's just that you should hold up your end of the bargain as well.

Tragically, since I had failed to take Laurel's advice to get Guru's offer to finance my own beauty business in writing, I was up shit creek on that one. I learned from that $5 million mistake to demand signed contracts for even the smallest promises.

However, Silver Palace did say I could take the Kmart deal elsewhere. That was huge. Now that I had permission to carry on with the Kmart deal, I had to figure out a way to structure it. Obviously, the Sikhs weren't going to be around to produce the private-label beauty products for Kmart, so I had to move quickly to fill the gap. The deal had grown to fifty-five private-label items, and I wasn't about to let ten months of work, including fifteen trips back and forth to Chicago, go down the drain just because Guru had become a corporate asshole.

I called one of my most important vendors: a company called Compound Consultants, which had been working with me on the Kmart deal from a different angle. You see, there's a lot that goes into structuring a project of this magnitude. You have to first put some formulations together. Then, you storyboard the product line and create a marketing plan. What Compound Consultants did was design the sets for all the displays. All of this has to happen before you are ever awarded the work in the first place.

Sets are like the custom display shelves and designs inside every store. In my opinion, Compound Consultants had done an unbelievable job. I mean, the shelving sets alone were drop-dead gorgeous. Compound Consultants had also been working on a project to actually build the shelving material itself. Winning a contract like that would be really lucrative, because we're talking about thousands of locations across the United States.

Once the guys at Compound Consultants heard I had been fired, they began to really freak out. After all, they had a huge investment in this deal and were terrified it would crumble. Well, Vinny to the rescue. I calmed them down and explained how we could still be awarded the business. It was simple. I would come work for them and do exactly what I had been doing.

"But, who is going to produce the beauty products?" one of the guys asked.

I had always known that the manufacturing of the beauty products isn't the hard part; it's winning the contract for the private-label placement in the first place. "Don't you worry yourself," I said. "I've got contacts all over the beauty industry, and I can find a high-quality manufacturer in no time."

And, I did.

Compound Consultants then asked me to start pulling over the business that I had developed. So, that's what I did. I went to Kmart and *wooed* them on board. Then, the fun really began.

What we had to figure out next was financing. A deal of this size takes a crap-ton of money to front. Once you are awarded the business, you can't then expect Kmart to hand you a check for half a million dollars so you can get things started. You have to have your own money so you can start the production of the products. Sadly, as good as I was at obtaining financing for huge corporate deals, I really sucked at handling my personal finances and getting backing for my own line.

It was about to get ugly.

Storming the Castle

There's a line in the movie *The Princess Bride* where the actor Billy Crystal says, "Have fun storming the castle!" Well, that was me. I headed back to Chicago to try to storm the Kmart castle, i.e. the giant Sears Tower. The building is at least a hundred stories tall and three hundred billion square feet in size. Well, okay, maybe I exaggerated a tad, but when you are inside of it, it sure feels that big.

After the attacks of 9/11, the building itself had become a fortress. The security was so tight, they required your entire handprint just to get in the front door. It was nuts, but this was *it*. This was go time! The last and final hurrah.

It came down to a one-day showing wherein each vendor would

make their final pitch. The winner of the bid would reap the rewards—a signed contract—and I was hell-bent on coming out of that gargantuan building with that contract in my hands. I was representing Compound Consultants, and we were bidding against three other competitors. If you've never seen something like this unfold, it's unreal. You and your competitors are all there at the same time. They keep you in different rooms. I don't know, maybe they think that if they put us all together, it would be like throwing a bunch of Dungeness crabs into a bucket: if you leave them in there too long, they'll start to eat each other.

The Kmart buyers went back and forth from one room to the next. Each time they came back in, they beat me up on cost and timing of delivery, as well as any other thing they could think of. It was tough, but what expedition to the summit of Mount Everest isn't? Believe me when I tell you, the size of this Kmart deal was the Mount Everest of beauty. On top of the typical competitors, there were a couple of Chinese vendors, too, which had me nervous. God love them, but dammit, those guys could bring down costs like seasoned hagglers at a flea market.

Since I wasn't allowed to talk to anyone outside my room, I constantly second-guessed myself. *Did the Chinese vendor really just lower the price that much? Did that New York vendor really just offer to do the sets and shelves for free? If the pope does shit in the woods, is that really necessary? I mean, doesn't the Vatican have indoor plumbing?*

In tense situations, questions like these swirl in your mind.

Finally, after a ten-hour marathon, I was mentally exhausted. The Kmart buyer came back into my room and took a seat. He sat there in his $2,000 Armani suit and just stared at me. I was doing anything I could to try to read his expression, but it was like looking at a brick wall. In the tension, I swear, I almost peed on myself. Then, he opened his mouth.

"The contract is yours."

My mind blanked for a second. I hardly knew what to say, so I just sat there, overwhelmed. I think he understood. I was excited, and I had a right to be. It was a $25 million contract, and $3.5 million of that money was mine.

He just smiled at me. "I'll be honest with you, Vinny," he said. "Yours wasn't even the lowest bid, but in the end, I just felt that with your experience, you were the right person for the job." He explained that they had to go out and get bank loans next, and then we'd start putting everything together.

When I called the guys at Compound Consultants to tell them the good news, I swear, I think they *did* pee on themselves. This was, by far, the largest deal they'd ever been a part of. Not only that, but in the next few days, Compound Consultants further agreed that they would back me as I launched my own brand. I was pumped! I couldn't believe it. To win the Kmart deal was awesome beyond anything I had ever known, and now I had my financial backing as well? Holy crap!

My next move: get that promise in writing!

I walked out of Sears Tower having just stormed the castle and won. I was on top of the world, and nothing could stop me.

I was so excited, I wanted to grab the first person I saw on the Chicago sidewalk and kiss them on the lips. Man or woman, I didn't care. But, this was Chicago, mind you, and I didn't want to die, so I squelched my enthusiasm. I was now 100 percent sure that I was going to launch my own brand. Compound Consultants was completely behind me, and after all, why wouldn't they be? I had just secured the biggest deal in their history.

Back home, I sat down with my attorney and talked about the fact that Compound Consultants wanted to back me. We drew up the paperwork for them to sign.

Some time went by, and we were now down to T-minus two days and counting toward Compound Consultants receiving the check from Kmart. Two days, two more measly days, and the order would be ours. I was so excited, my insides felt all discombobulated.

That's when it happened. The assholes fired me. Yeah, I just said that. Compound Consultants actually *fired* me. You see, they had figured out that if they fired me, they wouldn't have to pay me my commission. That little detail wasn't in my employment contract with them.

Mic drop.

I was stunned, to say the least—so stunned, I didn't even know how to get mad yet. It was all too shocking. Rest assured, a few hours later, it hit me freight-train style. I became furious. I wanted to hit someone or something—anything! And yet, I had no outlet. My contract with Compound Consultants was limited to when I was working for them. Since I was an independent contractor, it didn't cover what would happen if they decided to be the biggest dicks this side of the Mississippi River and fire me.

It remains one of the biggest betrayals of my life, along with Silver Palace.

Stuck, Stuck, Stuck

I don't know which was worse: the trauma of all the physical pain from pancreatitis, the plastic surgeries that had failed, the emotional trauma of having the person I love break up with me, or having just been royally screwed out of the commission check of a lifetime. Collectively, it was all too overwhelming.

I was really upset. My mind couldn't focus. Thankfully, my friends saw what was going on and were so supportive. I think they all knew I was in a really bad place emotionally. Thank God, Laurel came over, then both of my parents flew out from New Jersey to stay with me for a couple of weeks. Yet, even with all of that support, for the longest time my brain wouldn't process rational thought. I was in a deep, dark place and couldn't figure the way out. The more time that passed, the deeper the hole became. The hole was so deep, I didn't even consider more plastic surgery.

Since I had hit rock bottom, I knew that I needed a "reset." I mean, I felt worse than I had when Rob died. I wasn't eating. I wasn't sleeping. My friends knew something had to be done. Then, one of my friends made a suggestion to check out this clinic.

Enter the Hoffman Institute. Hoffman is the kind of place that is part clinic, part boot camp, and part resting zone. They help everyone, from those who have undergone trauma in their lives to business leaders wanting to become more focused in their thinking. The people and the experience at Hoffman would go on to change me.

I didn't realize it at the time, but the day I walked into the front door of Hoffman was my "reset" button. It marked the beginning of the rest of my life.

Hoffman's program of self-discovery is located in Saint Helena, California, in the Napa Valley. To this day, the Hoffman Institute represents one of the most important turning points of my life. They helped me understand how my thinking had been formed and how it was impacting my day-to-day life. They have what they call the "Hoffman Process." It's a seven-day soul-searching, healing retreat of transformation and development targeted to people who feel stuck in their lives. For me, it was more like stuck, stuck, stuck.

Some of the key things they help people work on include *making peace with the past*. Ah, yeah, I had a whole crap-ton of stuff to make peace with. They help *release you from negative behaviors*. Wow, I could write a book on that one. (In fact, since you're reading it, you know I've already done that.) They help with *emotional healing, self-forgiveness, and forgiveness of others*. At that point in my life, I had so many things to heal from and forgive myself about, I didn't even know where to start. Finally, they help you *discover your authentic self*. This one really solidified not just who I was as a person, but who I understood myself to be.

Before I got there, I didn't really know what their Process would be. There's a lot of information on the website, and my friends told me more, but the actual life-changing experience seems to defy description. Simply believe me when I say I am so glad I went.

Upon arriving, I had already filled out all the paperwork, and it was hard-core. Since I'm dyslexic, it was damn near impossible to complete. Not only that, but the terminology they used on that paperwork included words I had never heard before. They asked questions covering everything from childhood experiences, to medical history, to family dynamics. It took me an entire week just to get it done. Not to mention, Hoffman is expensive. Writing that check hurt a little, but had I known how powerful and life-changing the experience would be, I would have given them five times as much. Just don't tell them I said that, okay?

As I drove my Mercedes into Napa Valley that morning, everything outside my windshield became more and more remote. I mean, Saint Helena is located about half a mile from the middle of nowhere, so all you can see are hillsides and wine vineyards in every direction. Don't get me wrong, though. The area is freaking beautiful. Yet, being that far up in the hills away from the glitz and glamour of the big city wasn't exactly my idea of relaxing back then.

I was very nervous when I arrived. I really didn't know what I had gotten myself into. However, I knew it was something I had to do. Bear in mind, up to this point in my life I was still a pretty snooty guy about the kind of accommodations I stayed in. Thus, when I pulled up and saw the place, I was like, "Oh, my God." The whole place was just a set of these little cottages. It wasn't what I had expected at all, and it didn't look like my kind of place.

When I opened my car door, I received my next surprise. You see, the area itself is known as White Sulphur Springs. That's because sulphur-infused water pours out from the natural springs in the area, giving off a rotten-egg smell. It pervades everything. Yuck! Thankfully, once I got away from the sulphur pool, the smell disappeared and I could appreciate the beauty of the forty-five-acre property, a natural sanctuary.

It might not have looked (and smelled) like what I had pictured in my mind, but I was determined to get on with it. I popped the trunk and proceeded to pull out my brand-new Louis Vuitton luggage. Oh, hell yes, I never travel without a good set of Louis! The stench of the sulphur was really so overwhelming that I picked up a piece of luggage in one hand and covered my nose with the other. I must have looked like the epitome of a stuck-up jerk.

I went inside and checked in. The first thing the lady behind the counter asked me caught me off guard. "What did your parents call you when you were a child?"

"Um, they just called me Vinny. Why do you ask?"

"Well, your time here should be completely anonymous. No other guests here need to know your true identity. Everyone will call each other by their childhood names, and please don't tell people here what you do for a living. All that will come out later in the week, but for a few days this anonymity will help everyone step outside his or her normal daily life and move into a more emotionally focused way of being." She handed me my room key. "We get started at seven a.m., prompt, so please be ready."

"Seven a.m.?" I joked. "Is the sun even up at that hour?"

She just smiled.

One thing that took me by surprise at Hoffman was *the rule*: there was to be no telephone calling or emailing. "What?" I said. "I can't talk to anybody at home? How about television? How am I going to know what happens on my soaps?" I was kidding, of course, but I don't think the lady at the front desk got that.

She smiled again and said, "Hey, you can probably use a digital detox, too." Later, I realized that *the rule* was likely in my application material, but I'm glad I didn't know before I came. I might have freaked out.

After checking in, I pulled my car around back and saw that several other people were already there. As I later learned, we would all go through the Process together.

The next morning, we got started. I had anticipated that they would have me work on all these dysfunctional relationships I had experienced over the years. I mean, that was my problem, right? Boy, was I wrong. They reminded me that all that pre-Process work I had done a few weeks ago was, in fact, a whole work-up related to my parents. *My parents? What do my parents have to do with it?* I wondered.

Actually, the whole program operated under a philosophy, and it's one you might not initially agree with: our emotional issues begin in childhood due to the way we bond with our parents, and whether we emulated them or rebelled against them.

That was hard for me to stomach, because it sounded like blaming my parents.

Yet, that's only half of their philosophy. Yes, your parents are

100 percent involved, but they are NOT 100 percent to blame for who you are. *To blame*. Those are powerful words. Basically, it all boils down to how your parents raised you. Everything goes back to that. However, just because you were raised a certain way doesn't determine how you'll live your life. It's all about your negative emotional patterns, and my life had been full of them: grandiosity, attraction to the wrong type of guy, lavish spending, and obsession with love interests, to name a few. Hoffman helped me break those patterns.

Along the way, I began to realize that the way I am wired is in fact very correlated to how I was raised. That knowledge gave me a kind of *absolution* from my long-term patterns and behaviors. I began to see that this was learned behavior, and maybe I could change it. Without this Process, I never would have been able to see the framework of my life in terms of the experience I had with my parents. It was just where I needed to go.

I think back to some of the incredible people I met at Hoffman. I remember Nancy and Janis, whom I met first. I think what stood out in my mind was the way they looked at me when I first pulled up. It was pretty funny. They both had this look on their faces like, "Who the hell is this guy showing up in a Mercedes convertible, wearing the fancy clothes, and carrying Louis Vuitton luggage?"

I smiled at them and introduced myself. Don't get me wrong, they were really nice people, but Nancy looked at my white clothing and said, "Do you not know we're also going to be tromping around in the woods while we're here?"

"The woods?" I said. "You mean like, *outside* in the woods?" I looked at the trees in the distance and said, "Huh. Maybe we'll run into the pope out there and find out if it's true." I sat there with a straight face and waited to see if they got it. It took them a couple of seconds, but then they burst into laughter. That broke the ice and set the stage for our relationship during our visit.

Anyway, on my first morning, after a phenomenal breakfast, we introduced ourselves. We used our childhood names and spoke briefly about the pain that had brought us here. Now, like I said, Hoffman brings in people from all over the world with all types of backgrounds, including some very ordinary business types. I was surprised to see that in my group of thirty-nine, there were some "normal" people who had been through real hell.

We all made a pledge of confidentiality so every person in the room could feel safe as the veneers fell off, and people were honest— as honest as it gets. Some had had a loved one murdered, some had endured rape or molestation, and others were recovering from drug addiction. As we went around the circle, each took a turn to tell the others why they were there. I was the last to go. I sat there almost shaking my head.

I said, "Well, after listening to you all, I'm kind of embarrassed to say why I'm here." I mean, how could I not be? These people had gone through events that made my piddly little problems seem trivial.

"It's okay, Vinny," the counselor said. "We're all here together."

I exhaled. "I'm here because my parents loved me too much. They smothered me with love, and now I'm devastated trying to get over a boyfriend." I felt like a deflated helium balloon. For those first few days, I thought I was wasting their time because I didn't have a "real" problem. I was soon to find out that I had a very big problem, indeed.

Did Someone Die?

J ust how big of a problem, I didn't yet know, but from then on, everything they had us do was unexpected and new to me. They explained, "We're going to be searching for our quadrinity."

"Our quad-what?" I asked.

"Our whole self—our physical self, emotional self, intellectual self, and spiritual self. All occur interactively."

"Um, yeah, sounds great," I said, but quietly wondered, *What the hell are they talking about?* Believe me, the whole process of finding these four and then integrating them into one "whole self" was brand new to me. It was as mysterious as anything I've ever been through, but deeply rewarding.

One of the first things that we did was start unpacking who our parents were. What did they do? How did we interact with them? We were constantly looking at negative patterns and asking, "What character traits do you share with them?"

We started by trying to visualize our parents at home and "observing" them as they went about their lives. It's amazing in guided visualization how things come together. Next, they had us extract the negative patterns we all might have and figure out which ones are connected to us. When we wrote those negative patterns on big index cards, I ended up having around thirty. One at a time, we placed the index cards onto pillows and proceeded to beat the crap out of them with Wiffle bats. I mean, we beat our negative patterns until the cards had nearly disintegrated. (As you're reading this, you might be thinking that this all sounds stupid, but it wasn't. It was the most cathartic, liberating thing I had ever done.) For some, this was a really emotional experience. I didn't realize just how emotional it would be until, just before we started, one of the counselors handed out foam earplugs.

"What are these for?" I asked.

She smiled and patted me on the shoulder. "Well," I was told, "it could get a little loud in here and be distracting for some folks."

Boy, was she right. As people started beating their negative patterns, some began shouting and even crying. It was the most powerful and heart-wrenching group experience I ever had. Together, we were all fighting for our personal freedom and dignity.

Everything was very, very structured, right down to a curfew when we had to be in our rooms, and every day at Hoffman was different. We worked from 8:30 a.m. until 9:00 p.m. with regular breaks and meals, which were, by the way, wonderful. I gave them a five-star Vinny rating.

It was extremely challenging to talk about personal things with strangers. However, it became easier as we drew closer to one another and realized that this was a safe place to be vulnerable.

On another day, we each picked out a little pillow. Each pillow was formed in the shape of a baby and had a bow tied around it. I picked mine up and quietly said, "Please don't tell me we're supposed to beat this baby to death."

Thank goodness, it was nothing like that. The baby pillow was used to take us through various meditations about our parents. For example, in one meditation, we first pictured ourselves holding our mothers as children. Then, we tried to put ourselves in our mothers' shoes and think about what she must have felt with her parents. We worked all the way up through our mothers' lives that way, and came out of it with a profoundly compassionate understanding of who our mothers were and how they became who we knew today.

The most powerful meditation for me was when they had us imagine both ourselves and our mothers as children talking together as friends. This was truly amazing, and I learned so much about my parents and about myself.

Yet, it was the day we worked on our relationships with our fathers that really got me. I had never realized how much I thought I had disappointed him. I had no idea any of this stuff was inside of me. For you, as you read this, it's just words on paper, but to me, this was visceral. This was life-changing.

Prior to Hoffman, I had been so confused as to what my connection had been with my dad—the whole gay issue, and how I felt I had disappointed him. I began uncovering things buried deep inside that I didn't even know were there. The Process brought me full circle, as I moved from anger all the way back around to compassion, forgiveness, and love. Yes, there were times when I felt drained, but then I began to notice that my resiliency was really increasing. I was bouncing back pretty fast, and my lows were getting shorter and shorter.

Suddenly, I looked up and realized that all of us had been brought to a place where we were more open and loving with ourselves and each other. Hell no, we weren't all smiley and lovey-dovey, but we were more present and real without having to put up false fronts.

During the course of this week, one person left. I don't know why, but it was handled well. If I could wish anything for that person, it would be to urge them to come back and finish the Process.

As well as everything had been going, I unfortunately started getting pissed off, thinking, *What the hell? I came here because of Noah and Rob, and these people aren't even addressing my real-life issues.* Others were saying the same thing. Little did I know at the time, but by doing all the background stuff, I *was* addressing the issue of Noah and Rob. It began to dawn on me that maybe I was wrong. The process of identifying dysfunctional patterns, like the reason I started pulling out my hair, was a direct path to understanding other patterns in my life. Just when I thought I understood everything, I learned how wrong I had been.

The next morning, we went on a field trip of sorts, and remember, it's not as if I'd packed hiking boots in my Louis Vuitton luggage. So, on the hike, I wore my Guccis. That didn't make my feet feel great, but I was on this Hoffman thing for a reason, and I had no intention of quitting.

We visited a lovely remote cemetery nestled into the hillsides overlooking the valley below, where we sat and watched the sun rise. It was a beautiful, completely silent moment, one I'll always remember. The air was crisp with morning dew, and everything smelled fresh, like the aroma of freshly turned soil mixed with ground sage.

"Take a long walk through the cemetery until you feel drawn to a headstone that calls to you," said the counselor. "Imagine that your parents are in their graves, and speak lovingly to them about anything that is in your heart."

I was dubious, but took a leap of faith and just did as I was told. I spent what seemed like a long time walking, and at last, I found a headstone I really liked. It was old and a little crooked, and for some reason it felt comfortable to me. They even gave us flowers to place on the graves. For me, this was one of the most intense and emotionally cleansing experiences of my life. If there is such a thing as forgiveness and love, I experienced it here.

We spent the rest of the day and night in silence, and for the first time since I'd arrived, everything began to fall into place about what we were actually doing and why.

A couple of days later, at the end of our time together, we took the note cards on which we had written down our bad traits, and threw them into a fireplace. As we watched them burn, we stated what we had learned. It was literally a fire ceremony. We also did a final exercise where the emotionally hurt child we once were matures and integrates with the other aspects of our quadrinity to become a loving, whole, and resilient adult. As all things at Hoffman, this, too, was profound, and I can happily say I've never reverted back to the old Vinny.

I had come in with major issues: my unhealthy relationships, having been loved too much by my parents, trying to buy love with stuff, and changing my physical appearance through plastic surgery. The life-transforming thing I discovered there was that I should never again let anyone use me. Never, never again. I needed to value myself first and not try to buy people's attention. I needed to discover the beauty within.

No matter what we were at Hoffman for, by the end, it was addressed in a very individual way. Every person there was changed forever, and the people I had met were incredible. We had formed the most pure, unbiased friendships I'd ever had. We had this Process in common, and that remarkable opening up that we shared has stayed that way over time. Everybody stayed in contact afterward, and even years later, we still check in with one another periodically. Many Hoffman people are still in my life, and there are six or seven of them whom I talk to on a weekly basis.

I treasure my experience at Hoffman, and I wouldn't trade it even for a new set of Louis Vuitton luggage.

Train Wreck

After returning from Hoffman, I took a few days to regroup before I set out to look for employment opportunities. What better way than by reaching out to my connections in the industry? One was another beauty-industry vendor whom I'd prefer not to name, and after I tell you why, you'll understand. This vendor was a supplier to the beauty industry specializing in packaging design, manufacturing, and formulation for the mass market. She really knew her stuff. Let's call her "Ashley."

Ashley was what you'd think of as the prototypical Orange County, California, woman: tall, blonde, and trim, the result of lots of plastic surgery, including huge fake boobs. She always dripped in gaudy, oversized, and extremely overpriced jewelry. Oh, did I mention that she drove a Bentley? Believe me when I tell you, when

Ashley walked by, men turned their heads. Well, the ones who weren't gay did, anyway.

Although I'd never worked with Ashley or her company before, her reputation had preceded her. She had been with her company for twenty-five years, a lifetime in the industry, and she was the only woman on their sales force. Ashley was known as a rock star, a legend, and her success encouraged other women to follow her lead.

By the time we reconnected at a trade show after my stay at Hoffman, she had gone out on her own and started her own distributorship. Typically, as a distributor, you don't really develop anything. All of your products are pulled from different sources, and you distribute them to various buyers. Ashley, however, had bigger ideas.

The two of us really hit it off. I made it clear to her that I, too, wanted to do my own thing and not work for someone else. That really resonated with her, because she was the same way. She had become tired of working under someone else's thumb.

I had really come a long way in my knowledge of cosmetic chemistry by working with companies large and small. The more we talked, the more we connected. I told Ashley I wasn't really interested in working for a distributor, but she let me know she was getting ready to open up a laboratory. Since I wanted to focus on cosmetic chemistry, I got really excited.

She said, "We're opening up a new facility. Would you be interested in partnering with us to help us get the lab open?"

Well, now things were getting interesting. *Partnership?* I thought. *Hmmm, that just might work.* Besides running the lab, one of the things Ashley wanted of me was to bring over my existing white-label and budding private-label businesses. Normally, I would have been hesitant to do that for another employer, but since I would be a partner, it made a lot of sense.

We seemed to be perfect for one another. She had the distribution channel, and as an equal partner, I could develop our own proprietary product line. Although there was a twenty-year age difference between us, we had a lot of things in common, namely that she had been raised Polish Catholic and I was raised Italian Catholic. Our relationship seemed meant to be.

I made it very clear to Ashley that I had already developed my own brand and it was ready to go. She seemed dazzled with me, and to tell you the truth, I was dazzled with her as well. We were so alike in so many ways that I thought we were practically the same person. The negotiation of exactly what the partnership would be like took a couple of months, and in the end, the deal was that I would help Ashley's company build their brand first, and then turn my attention to my own. Ashley's husband was to be the chief financial officer of the company, so it was really the three of us. Let me tell you, Ashley was a woman who understood beauty, and she had everything I needed in-house.

One of the first things she wanted me to do when we began was to change my email address over to our company's email system. Honestly, I was so busy getting things going that I kept putting it off. I mean, first things first, right? In my mind, the first thing we had to do was get the lab open.

I helped them find laboratory equipment, testing equipment, ovens, and even the table for the conference room. I did it all. Even though I was becoming a decent cosmetic chemist myself, I wasn't cocky about it. Cosmetic chemistry is a huge area and unbelievably technical. I knew we needed a master chemist, so I found us one.

In the meantime, many major players who had worked with me in the past didn't seem to give a damn whether I was with Silver Palace or the new company. They commissioned me to create a gift basket of beauty products for Costco, develop a line of baby products for Safeway Inc.'s 1,200 grocery stores, and work on a private-label line for a big account in Texas. Once we got rolling, I made more money than I ever had.

Ashley soon became a conundrum, though. She was brilliant at business, but she was also one of the biggest gossips I've ever known. I mean, there were at least two or three hours a day that she would waste by gossiping to me. After a while, she started talking about the problems in her marriage. Ashley, being a really emotional person, was always crying about stuff. When you combined that with the knowledge that she was the consummate narcissist, you can see how things could get dicey.

As she confessed her innermost thoughts to me, I ended up doing the same. That meant I gave her an earful about the Noah debacle and how he had broken up with me by letter after I was hospitalized with pancreatitis. She was appropriately horrified and sympathetic.

Our relationship only deepened from there, and she wanted me closer to the business. Since Ashley's offices were located in Southern California, that meant I was driving my ass off to get there every day. Finally, I agreed with her. I moved out to a gorgeous place in Laguna Beach. The town kind of just called to me. It was expensive to lease, but that was okay, because I had money coming in. I thought I had left all my baggage behind.

Well, no sooner had things in my life started to stabilize when I met another guy. It was time to usher in the era of Zack.

My First True Love

Zack was another guy I met online, and it would be my first real two-way relationship. Well, maybe my second if you count Noah, who told me he loved me (once).

Around this time, Ashley began taking more and more of an interest in my personal life and my developing relationship with this new guy. You see, Ashley's relationship with her husband had started to deteriorate, and since she and I had gotten quite chummy, she told me *everything*. It was a lot to take in. She thought my burgeoning relationship was the greatest thing in the world and even encouraged me to go meet Zack in person in New York, where he lived. In fact, she set up some business calls for me so that the whole trip could be written off.

At the time, it just seemed like she was being ultrasupportive. I had no idea how far it would go.

Thus, Zack and I agreed to meet in person, and I flew from the left coast to the right. Now, even though I'd learned an unbelievable amount of things about myself at Hoffman, that didn't mean I had become instantly brilliant at self-diagnosis. My natural inclination upon arriving in New York was to book a fabulous hotel room at the Waldorf Astoria. I couldn't help myself. I wanted everything to be perfect for Zack.

And it would have been, had it not been for Ashley. Yes, Ashley. She kept calling me. I'm talking about every hour or two, my cell would ring. She wanted a minute-by-minute report. She even called at one in the morning, then three in the morning. It was nuts!

The night of my first date with Zack, the phone rang so often I ended up introducing Ashley to Zack over the phone. Can you believe it? She actually started crying to Zack about her marriage problems. I thought for sure that was going to scare him off, but Zack was amazing.

Well, you know me. I got a limo and had a dozen roses waiting inside for him. White ones, not red. See? I wasn't grandiose at all. Well, okay, maybe a little. I took him out to eat at the Four Seasons, where I had gone with my grandfather when I was a kid. Then, we took in a Broadway show before topping the night off with a horse-drawn carriage through Central Park.

The next night, I booked a helicopter tour over Manhattan. It dropped us off on the other side of the island, where we went to a restaurant and had caviar, truffles, smoked duck, and wine. When the waiter brought the bill, I almost fainted! Oh, well. So much for the avoidance of grandiosity. It was a fabulous evening!

When I got back to LA, however, things became increasingly weird. Ashley treated me as if I were her husband in every way but physically. As a result, her husband became more and more alienated. Lest we forget, he was a partner in the business, too! Ashley and I even started traveling together for business, leaving the poor husband to man the fort. At a trade show in Las Vegas, she was so attached to me that other people thought there was something going on between us.

Oh, crap. How do I get myself into these situations?

Since you've seen how nuts my life has been thus far, you might not be surprised when I tell you that I was then approached to be the focus of a reality-TV show. I'm not kidding. I had met a couple of the reality-show producers while they were filming another show at a friend's house, and that's where the connection began. They were interested in my life as a person, particularly my quest to start my own beauty brand. They saw it as the story of a true entrepreneur, someone who just wouldn't stop. Of course, they also liked the fact that I've had so many bizarre things happen in my life.

In retrospect, maybe the fact that a reality show contacted *me* should have tipped me off that so many areas of my life were still out of balance.

I was very excited about it and told them I had business partners around me constantly, so they'd have to be part of it. It didn't take Ashley and her husband more than two seconds to say, "Yes!"

The producers next told me that before we could jump into filming a reality show, they had to first put together what is known as a "sizzle reel." Sizzle reels are three- to five-minute-long videos that combine visuals, audio, and messaging to create a fast-paced, stylized overview of an upcoming show. They're kind of like proof-of-concept videos that are marketed to TV networks in the hopes of getting the presented TV show produced. Even though the division doing the filming had the same parent company, they still had to sell their concept to the network.

I thought, *Hey, great. I know exactly what we'll do for the sizzle reel. We'll hold an open call to find the spokesperson for my brand.* We knew it would make for great TV. You know, beautiful people all competing against one another for a chance to be a spokesperson. We couldn't miss! Ashley loved the idea, and so did the producers. Thus, arrangements were made to have fifteen guys and girls come by and be videoed talking about why they would be the right person for the job.

During the shoot, this one guy named Trevor came in. He was really beautiful. In fact, he was so gorgeous, he'd make a heterosexual man rethink his orientation. Both Ashley and I began flirting with him. It was hysterical. You can probably guess who got the spokesperson job.

Trevor and Ashley began cozying up immediately. With Ashley's marriage heading into the crapper, it became obvious she wanted to sleep with this guy. He was twenty-five years younger, but Ashley was so attractive that it was no surprise that he was interested in her as well.

Remember now, the guys from the TV show were there filming everything. So, they had the cameras rolling when Ashley started talking to me about Trevor. "Oh, Vinny. He just got into town. He was a marine and broke his knee, and he's been sleeping on people's floors because he has no place to live . . ." She went on and on. In short, she suggested that I have Trevor move into my place.

I thought, *Hey, what could go wrong?* Trevor's job would be to act as my personal trainer, in-home chef, and personal assistant.

Eventually, Ashley suggested that we do most of our work at my house instead of at the business office. Of course, Ashley had ulterior motives. She wanted a place away from her failing marriage to try to get Trevor into the sack. The production crew loved the idea. They were total professionals, so they wouldn't have said this out loud, but I could practically see them high-fiving each other. I mean, *this* was reality TV.

As you can imagine, things between Ashley and Trevor heated up. As part of the sizzle reel, I accepted an invitation to use a lake house from one of my friends at Hoffman. We took a bunch of friends there with us, and the film crew videoed everyone fishing and swimming. They got some great stuff.

Speaking of great stuff, they also found some real "reality" while at the lake house. Trevor and Ashley ended up in the shower together. Yeah, I know. It doesn't leave much to the imagination, does it? We're talking steamy footage here. And, she was still married! Her poor husband. But hey, the sizzle reel was certainly sizzling now. A cameraman came up to me and said, "Man, this is great stuff. We don't have to ad-lib. Your life is one big reality show!"

After that, my house became a haven for Ashley to come have sex with Trevor. Since she was so distracted by their affair, our business started sliding off. In the midst of all this, Ashley's husband became more and more suspicious.

From a business perspective, I was the linchpin holding the entire business together. Believe me, I did everything I could to keep it from falling apart. However, with Ashley spinning off the rails on one side and her husband spinning off the rails on the other, it wasn't easy. In retrospect, I don't know what Ashley was thinking. She was trying to keep her illicit affair a secret from her husband, yet the film crew was recording *everything*. Didn't she think her husband was going to watch the show once it finally aired? It was crazy.

Ashley was so torn about how to handle her screwed-up life that she would call me at all hours of the night and cry. The situation tore me apart, and eventually, even Zack complained. "Dude, with her calling all the time, there's no time left to talk to me." He was right. Managing Ashley and her whole situation had become my full-time job.

The night that Ashley went right the hell over the top, a delivery guy showed up at my house with a package for Trevor. When he opened it, I could not believe my eyes. The contents of the package turned out to be a set of car keys for a brand-new Acura. She had actually purchased him a $50,000 car. No joke. It was sitting in front of the house.

"Ashley," I finally said, "how do you think you're going to hide a fifty-thousand-dollar loan from your husband?" I mean, the business had pulled in a lot of money, but this was un-freaking-believable. Oh, and let me tell you, the film guys were eating it up!

A few days later, I went into the office to do a little work and Ashley's husband confronted me. "Is something going on with Ashley and another man?"

Finally, I was done—done covering for her, done with all her crap, and done with watching her destroy a business both she and I were working so hard to build. "Yes," I said. "She's having an affair with Trevor."

Naturally, the husband flipped out. He began throwing things around the office. What you might not believe, though, is that Ashley not only denied the whole thing, but managed to convince the poor guy that I had made it all up. In fact, when I showed up the next day, I was told that I didn't work there anymore. When I finally got Ashley on the phone, she acted like she didn't even know me. To this day, I've never heard from her.

To add salt to my wounds, Trevor continued to live at my house for another two or three months. Why I permitted it, I don't know. Maybe I had fallen off the Hoffman wagon briefly and reverted to my old ways of letting others take advantage of me. Let's just say that things were pretty tense. As for Ashley and Trevor, they did break up, but I heard they stayed in touch for years.

Again, you just can't make this stuff up.

And, do you know what turned out to be the smartest thing I did during that whole time? I had never changed my email address to the corporate one like Ashley had originally requested. So, I still had control of my email address book, which meant I still had control of my clients.

Ex-Squeeze Me?

s for the TV producers, they kept right on filming sizzle reels for my upcoming show. I permitted them, because the story, crazy as it was, would be great publicity for the company I was creating, TurnKey Beauty, Inc., a
research-and-development lab that would develop products for
businesses and celebrities. The name says it all. The company
would handle developing, testing, bottling, packaging, labeling,
global translation, barcoding, and distribution. It's a page taken
out of my mother's playbook when she had an all-encompassing
bridal business supplying everything from gowns to limousines.

My first major client was singer Lilian Garcia, a WWE announc-
er who came through a referral. She wanted a skincare line called
the "Surreal Star."

About the same time, Dayanara Torres, former Miss Puerto Rico, Miss Universe, and the first wife of singer Marc Anthony, was referred by Lilian. She commissioned a haircare line based on products indigenous to Puerto Rico. Talk about coincidences, because a few years later, I also helped develop a perfume named "Still" for Marc's *second* wife, Jennifer Lopez. Both J-Lo and Dayanara Torres helped put me on the radar for other celebrities, who came knocking on the door along with major clients like Disney, which commissioned a princess beauty set.

Through all of this, I also concentrated on Zack, the first healthy relationship I'd ever been in. It was loving in both directions, although Zack and I were still living on different sides of the country. Nevertheless, I was happy.

A couple of months later, I scheduled surgery to repair a couple of hernias caused by the pancreatitis I had endured. The hernias hurt like hell and had to be fixed. I never take surgery lightly, but to be honest, this didn't sound like a big deal. After all, I had gone under the knife for nearly thirty plastic surgeries before.

Damn, was I wrong! The surgery was scheduled to last an hour and a half. When I woke up nine hours later, I was horrified. "What the hell happened?" I said. "Why was I under for nine hours?" It turns out that when they opened me up, they found *eight* hernias, not two. I hadn't signed off on a nine-hour operation! You want to talk about painful? Holy crap.

A few days later, I was discharged. I had arranged for a nurse to come over and help me with the recovery. Little did I know that my recovery process was going to be hell on wheels. For the first couple of days, everything was fine, but then my belly button began to swell as if it were infected.

"Vinny," the nurse said, "we need to go to the doctor today."

I listened to her. The doc gave me a prescription for some antibiotics and smiled. "You'll be fine in a few days. Just head home and take these until they are gone."

However, by the next day, I was worse. After a few more days, the downward spiral had only continued. Damn! Luckily, I had made a friend at Hoffman who worked for the Centers for Disease Control and really knew her stuff. She took one look at me and said, "Vinny, you have MRSA. We're going to the infectious-disease doctor right now."

MRSA was one badass disease with which I was already too familiar. Remember, I had it once before. Usually, people contract this deadly infection in the hospital, and that's exactly where I had picked it up. Isn't that a nice little ancillary benefit of my hernia surgery?

The infectious-disease doc took about two seconds to admit me. He wasn't playing around, and frankly, the look on his face scared the crap out of me. After that, I had a virtual avalanche of medical people in and out of the room. One such physician came into my room and didn't introduce himself, but he looked like any other doc you might meet. You know, white lab coat, holding my medical chart, all that. He started asking me questions.

"How long have you felt this way?" he asked.

"What? You mean bloated, lethargic, sick as a dog? I don't know, I guess the last couple of days."

"No, when did you make the decision?"

"Decision? Doc, I didn't decide to get an infection. I had pancreatitis, which caused hernias. I just had multiple-hernia surgery."

He just stared at me, then he said, "I don't think we're on the same page."

"Tell me about it!" I said as I gave a little chuckle, but I could tell he didn't think that was funny.

"What I meant was, why do you want to have a sex-change operation?"

My mouth dropped open. "Ex-*squeeze* me?" I replied. "What are you effing talking about?"

The doctor looked back at the chart. "It says right here, GRS."

"What's GRS?"

"Gender-reassignment surgery."

I almost came off the hospital bed. The hospital had screwed up my chart! On one level, I could understand the mistake. The infection had swollen everything in my body, even my pectorals. In fact, my pecs were so enlarged, it made perfect sense. The chart said I wanted GRS, and my pecs resembled boobs. As a result, for the first three days they hadn't even been treating the MRSA. By the time their mistake was discovered, the infection had traveled throughout my body.

"Get that off my record right now!" I screamed. "Get somebody in here who knows what the hell they're doing!"

The physician ducked out of there with his tail between his legs. It wasn't long before the infectious-disease guy showed up and apologized profusely for his mistake. But, I was livid. My life was on the line.

As soon as I could, I called Zack. I was scared. When he heard the fear in my voice, he jumped on a plane. Given my history with men, that meant a lot to me.

I also called my parents, who still lived in our house in New Jersey. It hit them so hard that my father actually had what appeared to be a heart attack. They rushed him to the emergency room. Thank God it was angina, but his heart condition was so bad that the cardiologists decided he needed a stent. My poor mother was caught between being there to take care of my dad after his surgery and flying out to see me. My condition was so serious, there was a real chance I wouldn't survive. I think she was about to tear her hair out (no trichotillomania puns intended).

Since MRSA is so resistant, it can't be treated with regular antibiotics. Thus, they needed to give me a drug that doctors couldn't even prescribe, a drug that had to be requested and approved by the FDA. The reason behind this is because if it were widely prescribed, MRSA would become resistant to it as well.

My first bout with MRSA hadn't been as serious because they had caught it early. This time, however, the doctor's screw-up had cost me precious time, and time was not on my side. The approval process for the needed drug took a few days, and I began slipping into a coma. They rolled me into a plastic bubble to shield me from other germs. The MRSA infection traveled up my abdomen toward my neck. The next stop would be my brain, and then death.

Several hours later, Zack arrived. Up until that moment, he had had no idea that my condition was so grave that he would have to wear gloves, a mask, and booties. My memory is hazy, but I remember Zack losing it. After that, he really took control, talking to the army of medical people swarming around. Yet, there was nothing to be done until the drug came. My condition continued to decline.

I was in and out of consciousness, but I do have this one memory . . . more of a flicker, really. Thinking about it today gives me the shivers. It's of a Catholic priest walking into my room. The man administered last rites.

Man, I can't believe how close I came to death.

Zack broke all the rules when I was in the hospital. He literally gave me a manicure and pedicure while I lay in bed. He even put a mud mask on my face. He wanted me to look good in case I died. Talk about pursuing beauty to the extreme!

Needless to say, I was in considerable pain. The MRSA had affected my heart, liver, pancreas, and spleen, all of which throbbed within me. I was on massive amounts of painkillers, but nothing helped. One medication even caused hallucinations.

Still, the hard-core antibiotic had not arrived. In the early-morning hours of the next day, I remember hearing a helicopter. A nurse came running in and said, "That air ambulance is for you. Your medication is here!" I was too out of it to move, but Zack nearly jumped through the ceiling.

The physician bolted into the room with the IV bag in his hand. Within thirty seconds, he had hooked me up. All they could do at that point was wait. Within an hour, though, I began coming back. Not only that, but twenty-four hours later, the infection was 70 percent gone. That stuff is frigging miraculous.

By the time I was well enough to be discharged, I had spent twenty days in the hospital, and then I had to spend another twenty-five going back and forth for further treatment. Zack stayed at the house with me for a week after my discharge before going back to his New York college. Honestly, his loving care was literally the sweetest thing anyone had ever done for me.

Vinny and Marie

Some time prior to MRSA, I had been introduced to a chemist named Marie, who turned out to be one of the sharpest people I've ever known. I mean, she'd been a chemist for forty freaking years! We had never spent much time together, but we had a lot in common, including my friend Evelyn.

After I was out of the hospital, Evelyn asked me what I was doing for Thanksgiving.

"Zack is coming!" I said.

"Oh, that's great," Evelyn replied. "Is he staying for a couple of days?"

I informed her that not only was he coming for a few days, but he was also thinking about moving in with me and transferring to UC, Irvine, to finish his degree.

Since I was feeling nearly 100 percent, Evelyn and I decided to host this big Thanksgiving thing together. Zack was invited, as well as Evelyn's friend Marie, and we hit it off like two gal pals. I told Marie all about TurnKey Beauty and how I was creating private-label product lines. I also told her about my plans for my VS Vincenzo brand.

She listened intently, and I was truly star struck—or rather chemist struck—by her. Marie had a long and distinguished résumé and was what was called a "principal scientist," or one who researches natural ingredients for inclusion in new products. She had done everything, from the creation of the formula itself to helping sales and marketing teams with their presentations. She had also worked for big companies like Gillette and had developed a lot of the original shaving-cream formulations. Moreover, Marie had been instrumental in developing Earth Science's natural-beauty line, which is still sold in Whole Foods and health-food stores all across the country. In short, she was brilliant.

At the end of Thanksgiving dinner, she said, "Why don't you come visit my facility, Liquid Technologies?"

"How lovely!" I said. "Are you sure it would be okay?"

"Well, I'm one of the owners, so yeah, pretty sure," she replied with a little laugh.

When I eventually made my way over to visit her facility, she asked me a question I'd been wanting to answer for years: "What exactly do you want from a product line?" Up until this point, the only things I had done for my very own VS Vincenzo line were concept, art, and writing. Due to the lack of funding, I had never had a shot at producing a tangible line. Suddenly, everything became real. My goose bumps had baby goose bumps. Someone actually believed in me!

Although her company, Liquid Technologies, couldn't develop my product line for free, they were able to do some amazing things. They structured the deal to amortize a ton of costs, including Marie's fees, into what they were charging me. If they hadn't set it up that way, there would have been no way I could afford it. Marie took a huge leap of faith by supporting my dream. After all, if I flaked out or defaulted, her company would have been in a world of hurt.

Let me tell you, it's unbelievably hard to develop *one* beauty product from scratch. What we did over the next few months was develop *thirty-five* products for my Vincenzo line. That's not all. We developed another twenty-five for what I hoped would become my mass-market line, Aegean. It is a gorgeous line with packaging designed by Nolen & Associates. Unfortunately, it hasn't gotten to market yet.

During this time, I shadowed Marie in the lab to learn more about formulating products. I loved learning from her, and she seemed to love teaching me. I also developed all the packaging and graphics for VS Vincenzo, as well as the website. Then, we put together the entire package and started calling buyers.

It wasn't long before we realized we had too many products! There were so many to choose from that buyers were getting lost in the mix. Thus, we culled some, and that's pretty much what I did for a solid year, all the while still producing beauty products for the stars through TurnKey Beauty, Inc.

In time, Marie became part of my social circle and extended

family. She eventually sold her interest in Liquid Technologies and did consulting for a couple of years. I finally convinced her to come and work with me on my own business. Ah, true friendship is a beautiful thing!

We continue to work together to this day, and she's become a core part of my inner circle. She's seen me at my best, and if you must know, my worst.

So, that brings me back to Zack . . .

Zack Off Track

Zack moved in with me the May after Thanksgiving, when I first connected with Marie. We had some great times, but if I'm honest, we had some bad times, too.

His time was split between three things: classes at UC, Irvine, setting up an event-planning business of his own, and me. Unsurprisingly, he wasn't bringing in any real money, which meant that once again, I was sole breadwinner. Shit!

As for me, my finances fluctuated wildly. Being self-employed, it was either feast or famine. I admit, I didn't budget wisely. Oh, hell. I didn't budget at all! One day, we would go on a luxurious trip together, and the next week, when money ran short, we'd eat peanut-butter sandwiches. I was driving two cars, so on top of the house and living expenses, I had not one, but two car payments. I got so far behind that the bank sent repeated notices threatening to repossess both cars. What did I do? In typical Vinny fashion, I ignored them.

Despite the fact that Zack was incredibly nurturing and handled a lot of chores around the house, I began to resent paying all the bills. The house in Laguna Beach cost me a bloody fortune, and trying to fund the development of my line of beauty products cost me three fortunes. I was worried about money all the time, and took my frustrations out on Zack. It made for a tense household.

Despite all the tension, Zack really wanted to get married. For once, it wasn't me who was obsessed. So, even though I bought him a beautiful diamond-studded ring, I waffled.

Finally, Zack had a lightbulb moment. Even though his original plan after graduation had been to take his time finding a job, he saw how I was struggling. He began his job search immediately and landed at a wedding-dress company. Suffice to say, it wasn't his dream job. His next job was as the personal assistant to a high-profile, high-maintenance TV star in a hit show. He managed her professional and social calendars, ran errands, drove her around, and generally got stressed out. To make matters even harder, he had to drive two and a half hours each way in friggin' LA traffic to get to work. After a time, he decided to stay with a friend closer to his client during the week.

Suddenly, Zack's behavior shifted drastically. Instead of being this happy, fun-loving guy, I guess the stress of helping pay the bills for the first time in his life sunk in. He started drinking. It wasn't much at first, but it steadily increased over the next couple of months.

As I sit here telling this story, I can clearly see patterns in my younger years. Today, I can spot my own and other people's personality issues, but back then—even after Hoffman—not so much. Maybe I was attracted to guys prone to drug or alcohol abuse without even realizing it, or to people I thought needed taking care of. At any rate, Zack was sliding down that same path.

As time went on, he would go out and get drunk, then behave badly. When he would finally come back home, we got into big fights. He got so angry one night that he threw a bunch of my Baccarat crystal cocktail glasses across the room. It was a terrible, terrible time. From that point forward, Zack never really stopped drinking, and I never stopped trying to get him to stop.

After five years together, he told me he felt like California was killing him. He was done with all the faux stars and the glitz and glamour. He was also done with me. He wanted to do his own thing and move to Paris. (Like there are no faux stars and glitz and glam there?) I was crushed.

However, my angst over Zack paled in comparison to my mother's health. She was diagnosed with amyotrophic lateral sclerosis, better known as ALS, a motor-neuron disease. It caused her to fall one day and hit her head. She never came out of the coma and passed away five days before her seventy-second birthday. Her death hit me so hard that Zack decided to stay for a time, even going on to serve as a pallbearer at her funeral. After a time, and when I was more emotionally stable, he did end up following through with a civilized breakup.

Today, I'm thrilled to say that Zack eventually took hold of his life and is a productive and successful businessman . . . just not with me.

Star Power

Eighteen months after my mother's death, Dad was diagnosed with lung cancer, the result of a lifetime of smoking that began when he was in the US Army. Six months later, he passed away just prior to his seventy-second birthday, the same age as Mom when she died. Their passing left a hole in my heart that will never heal.

It took me several months of mourning before I rejoined the world. I devoted all my time and energy to my business, TurnKey Beauty, and it started popping . . . popping at the seams! I reached out to all my contacts, everyone I had built a relationship with over the years. It became my goal to meet new and exciting people.

This led me to some serious clients, and I signed five A-list celebrities. I was thrilled! Each of those celebs wanted what any good fashion icon wants: her or his own line of beauty products. Each contracted with me to design, formulate, and manufacture their own branded products. I was in beauty heaven!

As exciting as that was, wait until you hear this. My days of having a TV film crew around me were about to pay off. Without my even knowing it, the original sizzle reels had been circulated to various media outlets with the hope of landing a full-length show or even a series. Although the original concept never found a home, something even better happened. When the idea was proposed to a production company, they envisioned my story as a documentary that they temporarily named "The Science Behind the Beauty." They felt like my life and business were the perfect fit, and when they approached me about the idea of doing the project, I loved it.

We started making plans.

Even more amazing things started happening to me at the same time. Out of the blue, I was approached by *OC Metro*, a leading business magazine at the time. The editor came right out and told me that after all I'd accomplished that year creating cosmetic lines for the stars, they had chosen me as one of Orange County's "Forty Under Forty" people to watch. When I mentioned this to the guys at the production company, they loved the idea of opening their documentary with *OC Metro* doing the photoshoot of me for the cover.

After that, we started filming more of my business life, particularly my rise from nothingness into "the man behind the brands" of many larger-than-life celebrities. Of course, we also brought in aspects of my personal life. We even revisited things from my past, including *Dynasty*, the program that had fed so many of my early fantasies. To my delight, the production company arranged for us to use the actual house where *Dynasty* was filmed for a filming session. The film crew and I walked the grounds and even saw the lily pond where the very first catfight between Alexis (Joan Collins) and Krystle (Linda Evans) was filmed. To me, it was surreal—like seeing my pretend life juxtaposed on top of my real life. The producers even invited some of the cast of *Dynasty* to come be a part of the documentary, including actress Emma Samms, who had played Fallon Carrington Colby on the show. They told her how the show had shaped my life as a young child and how it had had an impact on culture in the '80s.

Emma was so gracious. She treated me like she had known me her whole life. And, here I was, this little boy from Vineland, New Jersey, who had grown up watching *Dynasty* with his grandmother. Meeting Emma Samms and several other cast members was one of the highlights of my life.

As filming of the documentary neared completion, I was able to think about everything it had covered. In retrospect, I was able to see that the production company's original idea for the documentary presented a really interesting contrast. It was a look at my business and life from the outside in, and *My Pursuit of Beauty* is a look at my life and business from the inside out.

DEVASTATION

Yes, indeed, things were definitely looking up—way up. I felt so good about my newfound successes that I decided to celebrate by getting a new dog, a beautiful English mastiff puppy I named Alexis, one of a series of dogs named after my favorite characters on *Dynasty*. (Doesn't everyone name their pets after their favorite TV stars?)

She arrived with an injured paw, so on Super Bowl Sunday, I took her to the vet. He treated her and told me to carry her around for a few days until the paw healed. What a great excuse to cuddle her all day long!

When we got back to the spectacular house I had leased in Laguna Niguel, I carried her in one arm as I went around the house lighting fires in the fireplaces and candles throughout. It was something I did for myself every day, whether or not I was expecting company. While lighting the candelabra on the grand piano, Alexis squirmed. That set off a series of fatal events.

My elbow hit the silver candelabra and it fell into the piano, immediately igniting. I dropped Alexis to try to close the lid and shut off oxygen to the fire, but in that split second, the flowing white curtains behind the piano burst into flames. In less than a minute, the entire room was ablaze, and thick black smoke billowed throughout the house.

I got down on my hands and knees and crawled around the floor calling out Alexis' name, only to realize that the poor pup hadn't yet learned it. Somehow I managed to dial 911 as I crawled from room to room frantically searching. I searched for Alexis until I couldn't breathe and couldn't see. Oh, the heat—I felt as though the skin on my face was melting off. *I'm about to die*, I thought.

Disoriented, I bumped into the French doors on the back of the house. Suddenly, the glass in the doors exploded outward due to the intense temperature in the house, and I was able to escape. I collapsed in the yard, coughing and gasping until paramedics arrived. They loaded me onto a gurney then headed to the hospital, sirens blaring.

Even though the fire department had arrived in record time, they couldn't save the structure and later determined that the temperature inside the house had been about 750 degrees. The only thing of value that survived the fire was my Maserati SUV Levante parked in the detached garage. I lost everything else: all of my carefully selected furnishings and decorations, original paintings, fine china and crystal, clothing. Not so much as a toothbrush survived. The things I mourned the most were the folded American flag from my father's funeral, his trumpet, a portrait of my grandfather conducting the symphony, pictures and videos of Teri and me growing up, and of course, Alexis.

Much later, when the structure was deemed safe to enter, firefighters found Alexis' remains. My only consolation was that she died of smoke inhalation rather than burning to death, a thought I couldn't bear.

Miraculously, I had escaped getting burned alive, but the smoke inhalation destroyed my esophagus and landed me in the hospital on a feeding tube for more than three months. When I finally started eating again, things didn't go well, to put it mildly. Instead of going to my stomach, the undigested food found its way into my lungs, and I developed aspiration pneumonia . . . repeatedly. When I didn't improve, they x-rayed and found the rotted food in my lungs. To save my life, I had a cutting-edge procedure performed called POEM (peroral endoscopic myotomy).

This could only happen to me, a person once so consumed with appearances that I had multiple plastic surgeries to improve my self-image. Now, I *needed* surgery to "improve" my insides, too. The doctors literally turned my esophagus inside out. Of course, in typical Vinny fashion, I developed complications from the surgery, namely psychological anorexia—a deathly fear of eating—which is a common reaction for people who are on feeding tubes for a long period of time. I lost one hundred pounds, and it took months of therapy to reeducate my brain to swallow again.

On the upside, so many of my friends in the beauty industry were wonderful to me during this time. It was extremely gratifying to have so many colleagues jump right in to offer tangible support. They brought me new clothing and even started a GoFundMe campaign to help replace my furnishings. In the interim, the insurance company put me up at a beach-resort condo for forty-five days, until I was able to rent a house not far from the one that had burned.

The house fire completely changed my life—not only physically, but psychologically. Having everything of value in my life literally go up in flames taught me that material things are ephemeral and can disappear in a flash, and that true friends will stand by you in good times and bad.

Visiting Angel

One of those friends-to-the-rescue was cosmetic legend Joni Rogers-Kante, the founder of SeneGence International®. She really went above and beyond to help me get through the aftermath of the fire. Her kindness and generosity should have come as no surprise to me, as she's one of the most wonderful people I've ever known.

Joni founded SeneGence in 1999 and quickly became a legend in the world of cosmetics. With that success came unscrupulous competitors attempting to pirate formulas for the very product that made her famous: her signature LipSense®, a long-lasting lip-color line with a three-coat application that comes in luscious colors and stays on lips for up to eighteen hours. When launched, it took off like a rocket and spawned an entire line of long-lasting products that stay put until removed. An element that added to her success was her business plan, a multilevel model designed for women who want to build a profitable career from home.

Enter Vinny.

We met in 2001, when I was working with a competitor who was trying to replicate Joni's exact formulations. Even though the two of us weren't yet acquainted, I felt compelled to "out" my client by going directly to Joni. I had heard nothing but good things about her, and I felt nothing but bad things about my client, whom I summarily fired. Monetarily, it wasn't my best idea, but honesty was an important part of my upbringing, and I sure didn't want to get a reputation as a corporate thief. Plus, working with even one crooked client could tarnish my reputation in the beauty industry forever.

Joni had heard rumors about competitors trying to duplicate her patented products, but until I came forward, she hadn't had a name to attach to the piracy. She thanked me profusely.

Never one to miss an opportunity to land a client, I told her I was a cosmetic chemist and offered my services. She gave me that "Maybe we can work together someday" line, which I had expected. After all, TurnKey was still a relatively new company with short-term clients. I was still searching for long-term business relationships.

Over the next few years, Joni and I bumped into one another at various cosmetic trade shows, and though we never really connected, SeneGence remained on my radar.

Many years later when I was on the prowl for new clients, I went to Joni's office without an appointment—my normal *modus operandi*—and told her I'd like to help reformulate her ten top-selling products. "I've been studying your product line," I told her, "and since trends have changed dramatically over the years, it's time for a major upgrade." She could have kicked me out of her office on the spot, but instead, she threw back her head, laughed, and agreed.

We clicked instantly.

Despite her colossal success, Joni had never had her own laboratory. So, I helped her design a small lab in the kitchen of a large building that would become her new headquarters. Joni and I worked together to reformulate her most popular products. The arrangement was ideal. She could visit the lab to check out my progress and be a part of the process while still running her business.

The new products were a hit, and the performance of their updated and trend-driven formulas exceeded the original. With the success of the products came a long-term consulting contract, and SeneGence became one of TurnKey's major clients. I also met with her distributors and helped her stage seminars for professionals, the same sort of thing I've done at TurnKey since I opened. One of my issues has been working for others, and the problem is that I've never wanted to sit in the back seat; I always want to *drive* the car. Owning my own company has allowed me the creative freedom I've always needed.

Actually, it's pretty crazy. At TurnKey, I'm involved in everything: billing, packaging, formulation development, research and development (R&D), and whatever else it takes to keep things rolling along. I'm also out in the public calling on potential clients, working directly with A-list stars, appearing on TV and the radio, and speaking at beauty conventions. I love every aspect of the business.

During the last twenty-five years, I've developed over three hundred brands that run the gamut from hemorrhoid salves to fine fragrances. Only twice in all these years has anyone ever acknowledged publicly that I created some of the leading formulations for their products. Joni was the first, and it sure as hell felt good to be recognized in front of my peers at major beauty events!

Beyond our careers, our relationship is also personal. During the years I was working with Joni, I lost my mom and dad in quick succession, and she and her husband, Ben, became surrogate parents to me. Being part of their nurturing circle was a Godsend. And, when I was battling my various illnesses, Joni and Ben brought me groceries weekly, along with a paycheck in the same amount I would've earned had I been going into her lab every day. They supported me until I was on my feet again.

Fast-forward three years, and although I no longer worked with SeneGence, TurnKey was thriving. I was living in the house of my dreams, and I was financially stable. Finally! Then came the fire that took me out of the game. Once again, without work, I couldn't pay my bills, and with the exception of the car, every single *thing* I cared about had been wiped out in a few hours. I had zero. Nada. Even though several years had passed since we worked together, Joni and I remained close, and she swooped right back into my life when I needed friends most. Once again, she and Ben brought me not only a paycheck—even though I was no longer consulting for her—but meals, too. Equally important, they brought me friendship, moral support, and laughter.

No one in my entire life has ever stood up for me like that.

In addition to being a client and friend, Joni has been a role model for me in so many ways. Whenever she walks into her office, smiles break out and employees are visibly happier. How many bosses can do that? Thinking back to some of the effing jerks I've worked for, hardly any. By emulating her style, I've made TurnKey a better place to work.

Simply put, Joni is my hero. In fact, she is a hero around the world. Her nonprofit, The Make Sense Foundation, helps women and children in need, and she lends her time and dollars to scores of other nonprofits, as well.

When I first met her, SeneGence was an up-and-coming company. Today, it's one of the world's most successful multilevel-marketing companies.

Coming Together

After all the ups and downs of my life—crazy bosses, multiple boyfriends, numerous surgeries, losing my parents and grandparents, and surviving the fire in the Laguna Niguel house—my life has finally come together. I'm at the cusp of a dream that began when I was nine years old. Back then I was watching soaps, drooling over the bigger-than-life characters on *Dynasty*, and concocting potions in whatever containers I could scrounge. I've never for a minute veered from my dream of owning my own cosmetic firm. It took years of working for free so I could learn the cosmetic business, followed by years of schooling and mentoring, but I learned it all. It was excruciatingly difficult and amazingly satisfying at the same time.

As soon as I hung out the TurnKey shingle, clients I had worked with at previous companies came knocking. When those first celebrities appeared on my doorstep, they graciously spread the word about me. TurnKey became *the* place for when stars wanted to develop lines under their own names. We also became the go-to company for top talent agencies like William Morris, APA (Agency for the Performing Arts), and CAA (Creative Artists Agency), all of which encourage their clients to put their names on cosmetic lines.

After reading this far, I hope you've become interested in knowing how this crazy business works. For starters, the beauty industry is obsessed with helping people look and feel beautiful. The industry has three designations of products: cosmetics, personal care, and fine fragrances.

It takes education, creativity, and hard work to develop even the most basic lotions and creams. First of all, for cosmetics and personal-care products, you need a background in chemistry. However, for fine fragrances and cologne, it's best to become a "certified nose." What is a "certified nose," you ask? Let me put it in these terms. The title "cosmetic chemist" is equivalent to getting a BA degree. A "certified nose" designation is equivalent to receiving another BA in perfumery, an entirely different field. It's just below the designation of "perfumer," the equivalency of a PhD in fragrances, and I'm working toward that goal.

Now, I'm not knocking a formal education, like the classes I took at UCLA, but that's just the first step to learning this crazy business. It was the on-the-job training at numerous beauty companies I worked with for over twenty-five years that taught me what I needed to know. However, the most valuable lessons were from my mentors, Marie Ardita and Lee Paler. These unbelievable people taught me how to develop complex formulas in the arena of haircare, skincare, bath and body, over-the-counter products (OTCs), baby products, and even pet products. Plus, they taught me the real-world skills I needed to run a business: marketing, packaging, sales, and leadership.

After that, I still wasn't quite ready to do everything needed in a full-service business. So, I got additional training at a local fragrance house, where I learned to identify fragrances by breathing them in. Honing this skill was important so I could become a certified nose and develop high-end fragrances.

Sound simple? Well, it's not. It's unbelievably hard work. That's why there are so few certified noses around. The training method used is much like the way sommeliers, specialists in the fine art of pairing wine, learn their trade. The reward came at the end of the term, when I passed all the intricate tests so my schnozzle could be certified. With this additional certification, I was able to offer TurnKey clients even more products.

How does a beauty company like ours make it all work? One word: slowly! Most celebs, entrepreneurs, retail chains, and corporate clients who approach us to have their product lines developed have the mistaken idea about the length of time the process takes. I tell them that a miracle-fast launch may be six months, but realistically, launches take more like twelve to eighteen months. We need at least four months to develop the formulations alone, then another ninety days for compatibility and stability packaging required by the FDA. And, that's only if everything sails smoothly.

Some of our clients look to us to develop products that are considered OTCs: sunscreens, hair-regrowth serums, hand sanitizers, and products that treat conditions such as acne, dermatitis, eczema, psoriasis, hemorrhoids, etc. These sorts of products have to meet even higher standards and go through additional screening and testing. With this in mind, it makes sense that these take longer for approval than cosmetics.

Then there's the process of cataloguing the ingredients contained in each product. It's mindboggling, particularly for someone like me with dyslexia. Luckily, Marie taught me how to do all the regulatory stuff and what we call "authoring the paperwork." To give you an idea of how much paperwork it takes, let's say a single product has thirty-five ingredients. Each is required to have a safety data sheet (SDS) and a Certificate of Analysis (COA). That equals up to seventy pieces of freakin' paper for a single product. Shit!

All of this is why TurnKey Beauty is a very boutique company; we only accept four to six clients every eighteen months. Believe me, that keeps us plenty busy.

That's not all. Once the client signs off that the products meet her or his satisfaction, there is another lengthy process of selecting bottles, containers, boxes, labels, and more. I can bring in samples for clients to see, but it's much more fun to take them to the glitziest, most glamorous trade show, where they can touch and feel more products in a single day than they ever thought existed. It helps them hone in on what they really want. Additionally, it gives us a chance to have "the talk" about pricing and what would work best for their needs. We also introduce our clients to our brokerage-and-distribution team, who help launch the product and do bar-coding and labeling in various languages to accommodate the foreign market.

There's more. A ton of my clients are stylists who hire me to create hair products to be used exclusively on their clientele, like Beyoncé, Madonna, and even Michelle Obama. It still gives me goose bumps to think that the former First Lady of the United States uses products we developed! Even back in my *Dynasty*-obsession days I never dreamed that big.

If you're wondering what the experience is like for my clients, it works something like this. On their first visit, I ask them to bring in several of their favorite products so I can get an idea of what they like. Let's say they have two favorite face creams, but one is just a tad too greasy and the other dries out their skin. What they want is a combination of the two. Like a detective, I reverse-engineer those products and break them down to find what I call "the offenders," or the problem ingredients. Then, I create a totally unique product.

The overall process is one of trial and error. Sometimes we do twenty or more submissions to clients, revising and revamping each one, before they sign off. They might want us to change the color or the fragrance of the product, or the way it feels on the skin. Does it dry too quickly or stay on top of the skin too long? There are a million things to consider.

Some clients know precisely how they want their products to look, smell, taste, and feel. Others just tell me, "Go at it." No matter what, we always recommend that a collection contain at least three or four products, because stores don't want to give shelf space if a line is not expansive.

Occasionally, a client will say, "I absolutely love what you've done here, but can you just change the color from pink to blue, or change the scent from lavender to citrus?"

I tell them, "There is no 'can you just.' Every ingredient has a different chemical makeup, and to make even a single change, we have to go back to the beginning and start over."

Therein lies the challenge.

For instance, Jessica Simpson—who is a total sweetheart, by the way—asked me to collaborate with other chemists on a line of edible beauty products. Sounds sexy, doesn't it? Well, that was the point. Her tagline for the product line was "Sexy Girls Have Dessert," and I just loved the concept. There was Whipped Body Cream with Candy Sprinkles, Hot Body Topping, Deliciously Kissable Belly Button Love Potion Fragrance, and Deliciously Kissable Lip Gloss. The flavors were amazing: Cotton Candy, Vanilla Cream, and Cinnamon Bun. Creating an edible product line was a first for me, and the creative process was a kick. The approval process? Eh, not so much.

Another project was working with Damone Roberts, a celebrity makeup artist, and it was a true collaboration. His specialty is eyebrows, and his list of clients includes the crème de la crème of Hollywood and beyond: Oprah, Madonna, Beyoncé, Rihanna, Kim Kardashian, Gwyneth Paltrow, Channing Tatum, Alicia Keys, Christina Aguilera, Nicki Minaj, and Robert Downey Jr., to name a few.

Damone presented me with a challenge. Instead of bottles or tubes, he wanted a line of facial wipes in sealed packets. His idea was that there would be four products: two for morning and two for evening. The morning wipes would wake up the skin and hydrate it. The evening wipes contained a makeup remover and a night cream.

The more we talked, the more exciting the idea became. After the tragedy of 9/11, procedures at airports had changed worldwide. With this in mind, Damone wanted a product that would pass through airport TSA security with the greatest of ease. No more worries about three-ounce containers in quart-size baggies to present at check-in, and no more worries about larger bottles breaking in checked luggage.

There was a lot of trial and error. We even had to hire a packaging engineer, a person who could help us manufacture a tool to put just the right amount of chemicals on the wipes. The end result was a product so novel that we applied for and received a patent. He named it AM•PM™, and it contains a proprietary blend of natural ingredients free of mineral oil, synthetic dyes, and other offenders. It hit the market in attractive black-and-white packets at just the right time in history.

Projects like these are really the dream, but they're not all that way. Some clients are A-listers who are terrific, but they hire incompetent people to manage their projects. One client (who shall remain nameless) was constantly on tour, but wanted a line of bright-blue cosmetic brushes. She hired four women to manage the process. I knew instantly upon meeting them that they would be PIAs (pains in the ass). They had demands far more complex than those the client had discussed with me. One such demand involved the Pantone Matching System® (PMS), the international color language used worldwide. PMS contains every variation on every color. The system is hundreds of pages long, and in my business, it's like the Bible. You can't go into production without a PMS number. None of the colors in the book suited these women, though. They wanted the exact royal blue used on Range Rovers that year. We had to request paint chips from the dealership, then spend months matching the PMS color to the paint color on a friggin' SUV.

But, there was yet another hitch. When they finally agreed that the color was a match for one in the PMS book, they looked at the corresponding PMS number and deemed it to be "bad luck." They insisted we keep searching for a number with "good karma."

"Are you fucking kidding me?" I blurted. It was beyond maddening.

The next problem was the brushes themselves. To give you the background, every brush, regardless of its purpose, has three parts: the bristles, the ferrule (the piece of metal that clamps the bristles), and the handle. Well, instead of leaving the thickness of the bristles to the experts, these women insisted that each brush have exactly 1,500 hairs.

Eighteen agonizing months later, I heaved a sigh, said a few choice words, and submitted the brushes for review. Even after all the craziness, I thought approval would be simple. But, no! One of the ladies actually took out a hammer and nailed the brush to a board. The four of them then spent two hours counting each bristle. I shit you not. The result was 1,487 bristles. They rejected the brushes.

That was the last straw. For the first time in twenty-five years, I fired the client—not because of anything she had done, but because there was no way in hell I was going to continue the madness of working with those four lunatics. There were plenty of great clients waiting in the wings for me to develop their cosmetic lines. It was past time to move on.

Where Dreams Meet Reality

D espite my success in developing products for celebrities, corporations, and retail chains, I'd always yearned to produce a cosmetic line under the name of VS Vincenzo. But, no ordinary product would do. It had to be an extravagant line (and why not?) that would rock the socks off the industry. I said to myself, "What would be the most over-the-top ingredients in the world?" Then, it hit me: caviar and diamond dust!

Caviar? That little jar of black fish eggs? Damn right. Caviar is not just edible; it's good for the skin. It has antiaging properties that diminish fine lines, wrinkles, and feathering. It also contributes to renewing and regenerating energy to long-forgotten skin cells. The end result is more youthful-looking skin.

Diamond dust, something called "sirt," also plays a key role in the antiaging process. Combine caviar and diamond dust, and you end up with products loaded with proteins, vitamins, and minerals. The combination is friggin' dy-no-mite.

So, after years of reformulating and testing to get just the right combination, my VS Vincenzo line of four products was ready. There's Dual Active Micellar Fluid (facial cleaner, toner, and make-up remover), Dual Action Face Crème, Morning Dew Drops (known as "Botox in a capsule"), and Dual Active Eye Crème. I named the line—what else?—Caviar & Diamonds.

However, before my products could debut, I had to find a company that could produce the product to my exact specifications, and fill the jars with the diamond sirt (dust) and caviar extract so tiny caviar beads could be seen within each jar. I refused to compromise. Unfortunately, the only American company that could do it was crazy-expensive.

I was getting discouraged, when I remembered a long-ago connection whom, believe it or not, I had met while working with Ashley, the Wicked Witch of the West. Years before, she had introduced me to a client named Violetta, who later formed her own skincare consulting-and-product-development company in her native Poland and named it Blushe.

Fortunately, she remembered me, so I flew to Warsaw to meet with her. The manufacturing company turned out to be a perfect fit for VS Vincenzo's first products. Violetta thought my formulation of the gelatin caviar beads that women break open and apply to their skin was brilliant. Her company had the proper equipment and technology to fill the jars in an aesthetically pleasing arrangement.

Plus, her cost was one quarter what it would be with the American company. We came to an agreement on the spot.

The cool thing is that not only does the arrangement benefit me, it benefits the Poles. They're thrilled to have new American business, and I'm thrilled to be a big fish in a small pond where they treat me like royalty.

Doing business in Poland has also given me a unique opportunity. Remember my obsession with WWII history, particularly the Holocaust? Well, Auschwitz, the most infamous of the Nazi killing camps, is located in Poland. While I was meeting with Violetta, I asked my hosts to arrange tours of the Warsaw Ghetto, the Holocaust Museum, and especially Auschwitz, the most "efficient" conveyor belt of death ever known.

For reasons unknown to me, Vinny, who is obsessed with beauty, is particularly fixated on Adolf Hitler. Not that I admire him. Hell no! *Hell* no! My preoccupation is trying to understand how a crazed psychopathic criminal rose to absolute power and carried out the most diabolically efficient mass executions the world has ever known. He was so "successful" that more than eleven million people from Europe, the Baltics, and Russia perished. Five million were non-Jews, and six million were Jews, who had been targeted for total extermination.

In earlier years, I read *Mein Kampf* ("My Struggle"), the book Hitler wrote during the three years he was in prison for high treason. I read it three effing times—not an easy task for someone with dyslexia. His diabolical plan was all there in black and white. Hitler not only described in great detail *what* he was going to do, but *how* he was going to go about it. And, damned if he didn't attract an evil group of henchmen led by Joseph Goebbels, Adolf Eichmann, Herman

Goering, and Heinrich Himmler, who carried out the atrocities and exterminations he had outlined.

The more I studied WWII history and reread *Mein Kampf*, the more obsessed I became with visiting Auschwitz to bear witness to the millions who had died there. Thus, when the opportunity arose, I wasn't going to let it pass me by.

Well, I think you probably know me well enough by now to know that I always go all out. I not only wanted to tour the camp, I wanted to stay overnight. And by hook or crook, I was able to get permission. So, once all the other tourists had left at the end of visitor's hours and the gates had clanged shut, an English-speaking guard approached me.

"Are you sure you really want to do this?" he asked. "We don't have food or blankets, and there's no bathroom."

I assured him I had every intention of staying, so he led me back to the barracks I had seen on the tour and gave me a walkie-talkie. "Use this if you decide to leave. I'll be on patrol all night," he said. I'm sure he thought I was a little daft, and honestly, I probably was!

To make the experience as authentic as possible, I handed him my cell phone so I wouldn't be tempted to use it. I even changed into pajamas, which I had brought with me in a briefcase, and took off my socks in order to mimic the prisoners' clothing. Before dark, as I sat down on the uneven wooden slats the Germans called "bunks," I tried to read the thousands of faint messages scribbled on the narrow planks and walls. Well, they were written in Polish, Russian, Hebrew, or German, and I, unfortunately, am not fluent in any. I wondered what they said. Did the prisoners leave warnings for others telling them about the slaughters to come? Or, did they simply write their names to leave some trace of their existence on earth?

By eight o'clock, it was dark, dank, and eerie, the way I had imagined it was most of the time. How could the sun dare shine on such an evil place? I've never believed in supernatural stuff, but I kind of felt that there were three million loose spirits whispering to me through the gathering winds.

The later it got, the colder it became, and at about two o'clock, the rain came. I'm talking monsoon, end-of-times thunderstorms. Torrents of rain poured through the roof and soaked me. To make matters even more miserable, the wind whipped up from the openings in the floor, which was set on pillars about two feet off the ground.

I'm guessing the temperature dropped from about fifty-five degrees to thirty-five. It was friggin' freezing. I had recently recovered from a bout of pneumonia, and for a nanosecond, I had a fleeting thought: *Am I crazy to set myself up for a relapse?* Then I muttered, "Shit. If I get sick, I'll just go back to the hospital. I'm not giving up now."

Sleep was impossible, and the night dragged on. Peering through the dark at row upon row of beds in the barracks originally built for three hundred, I tried to imagine what it was like when the population in each swelled to three thousand. I had read that the bunks were so crowded that prisoners could only sleep on their sides, spooned up against one another. The overcrowding had not only added to each prisoner's misery, it created the perfect storm for typhoid, dysentery, and lice. Prisoners were not only killed in the gas chambers, they died by the thousands of disease, all by Hitler's design.

As I lay there shivering, I thought about my past, my present, and my future. My entire life, I had been in pursuit of beauty. I had never been content with my looks, and had undergone multiple plastic surgeries to improve my appearance. Not only that, the single-minded focus of my adult life had been developing cosmetics to make other people look and feel beautiful. I had always indulged myself with expensive cars, lavish homes, and spectacular paintings. I had taken pride in being invited to parties with Hollywood elite, red-carpet events like the Oscars, and staying at only the most luxurious hotels and resorts when I traveled. Only the best would do. And, even though I love what I do and feel there's a need for beauty products, in that moment, everything in my past seemed unimportant and trite compared to the prisoners' suffering at Auschwitz and other Nazi extermination camps.

Despite all my efforts to create the most authentic experience possible, I felt inauthentic. Unlike the prisoners, I wasn't beaten and starved. In the morning, I could return to a fancy hotel, have a warm bath, and eat all I wanted. They, on the other hand, had been doomed, imprisoned. The only way out for most was the gas chamber.

I realized that there was no way to ever recreate that unimaginable time.

The guard came at about 7:00 a.m., ten hours after he had left me. He said, "I can't believe you lasted all night! My buddy tells me that out of the millions who have visited this camp over the years, only two hundred and twenty crazy people like you have ever wanted to spend the night. Only twelve have made it all the way through."

Of course, there was no way to verify what he said, but I suppose he had his facts right.

As we walked back toward the gate, I pointed out the thousands of tiny, yellow wild buttercups I had taken pictures of during the public tour. Their beauty seemed incongruous in this hellhole. What struck me most was that large patches bloomed over the execution pits, where the bodies had been burned and buried. A virtual yellow blanket covered the sites of the gas chambers. Curiously, all the blooms were *inside* the barbed-wire fence. The soil outside the fence was identical and got the same amount of rain, yet it was completely barren.

"Wow," he said. "I can't believe I've never noticed that before."

I turned to him and wondered aloud if the ashes, decaying bones, and flesh of the millions who had died there in the 1940s continued to enrich the soil, creating a modicum of beauty in a place of such ugliness. Maybe it was Mother Nature's way of marking the passing of so many innocent souls.

He nodded. "You could be right. There's no other explanation why wildflowers don't grow *outside* the fence, where there were no killings."

When I returned to the hotel, I sat on the side of the bed and tried to process the previous night. Despite my experience, I was no closer to understanding the minds of the Nazis than when I had entered. Just the opposite, in fact. I mean, the Nazis weren't alien monsters who came from other planets to massacre millions of earthlings. These real-life monsters set out to systematically destroy fellow human beings whose beliefs or nationalities were different from their own. Was their motivation unfounded hatred of anyone they deemed not to be Aryan, pure jealousy, or a desire to enrich themselves? Or all three? The history books are full of conjecture, but no explanation will ever justify their actions.

So, what does all this have to do with my continuing pursuit of beauty? Actually, it has everything to do with it.

Spending the night at Auschwitz was unequivocally one of the most life-changing moments of my life—even more than my grandmother's death and my time at the Hoffman Institute. It was like I was one person when I arrived at Auschwitz, and someone totally different the following morning. During those ten hours in the bunkhouse, I miraculously found that I had everything I needed within myself. I didn't need more plastic surgeries to improve my appearance. I didn't need a bigger house, better cars, or more stuff to impress people. For the first time in my life, I was comfortable in my own skin.

THE JOURNEY HOME

With the life-changing experience fresh in my mind, and the production of Caviar & Diamonds safely in Violetta's capable hands, I returned to LA to decide where to launch the very first products under the VS Vincenzo brand.

In a typical over-the-top Vinny move, I didn't want to launch in the US, because American women—even celebrities—are very price conscious, and because of the expensive ingredients, I needed to charge a hefty price. Ultimately, I decided to launch my line in the Middle East and Europe. Time will tell.

Why the Middle East and Europe, you ask? Well, believe it or not, women in Dubai, Tehran, and Kuwait City are the biggest consumers of high-end beauty products in the world, and they are much less price sensitive. Underneath all those burkas, jilbabs, and hijabs are some seriously beautiful women. They wear the best designer clothes and shoes, and insist on only the best and most expensive cosmetics in the world. The same can be said for European women. Who am I to deny them?

Upon making this choice, what I didn't fully realize was how difficult it would be to launch outside of the US due to the international process being a true mind-bender. Each country has its own version of the FDA that approves products, so I had to hire a representative in each country to squire the products through the approval process . . . one friggin' country at a time.

It can take four to six months, or even more, to receive the paperwork, add the bar-coding and artwork, calculate the pricing using the country's monetary system, and to have the labels translated into multiple languages—all just to get the products registered. So, I am not even permitted to give out samples at trade shows until all of this is complete. It's a huge PIA, but it is so worth it in the end, because it opens up markets worldwide.

Once Caviar & Diamonds is on prestigious retail shelves, the next VS Vincenzo products incorporating precious metals will follow close behind. Think rubies, emeralds, silver, and gold. They're all loaded with beneficial properties. We're set to go with a Champagne & Gold line next, which includes a fizz mask and a line-blurring product that diminishes fine lines and wrinkles on contact. The stuff is effing miraculous!

If you're wondering about the use of precious jewels, let me give you a mini chemistry lesson. Magnesium salts soothe and heal damaged skin, and pass through to the lower layers. Copper works with Vitamin C to promote the growth of elastin and collagen, giving the skin a more youthful appearance. It also stimulates enzymes that occur naturally in the body. Zinc acts as an astringent and helps prevent acne. It also helps keep excess oils from forming on the surface of the skin. The bottom line is, adding precious metals and jewel dust enhances the effectiveness of skincare products.

I guess when it gets right down to it, you just can't top Mother Nature.

Dynasties

So, how did I go from watching *Dynasty* as a kid to developing beauty products using precious metals? And, how are the two connected? I had never given much thought to the definition of the word "dynasty." It means "a powerful group or family that maintained its position of power for a considerable length of time." What resonated with me about the program was not the meaning of the title, but the over-the-top trials and tribulations of the not-so-nice Carrington and Colby clans.

Recently, it gave me pause.

Family dynasties are not only important to royalty, they're also important to mere mortals, like the Spinnato family. Therein lies the rub. Since I was my father's only son, I was expected to carry on the

Spinnato name by marrying and having a passel of Italian kids who would perpetuate the family name. That notion was shattered when I came out as gay as a teen.

Don't get me wrong—it came as no surprise to anyone, and my family was very supportive—but the Spinnato "dynasty" was running low on heirs. There were only two direct male descendants left. One was me, and the other was my cousin, Eric Spinnato. But, not to worry, Eric has boys, so the Spinnato name is far from becoming extinct.

Plus, I like to think there is more than one way to carry on a dynasty. Instead of through children, I hope my VS Vincenzo brand will follow in the footsteps of other great companies that have withstood the test of time. I'm talking about my favorite luxury brands that were named after their founders: Baccarat, 1764; Tiffany, 1837; Cartier, 1847; Louis Vuitton, who became a trunk master in 1859 (he's my man!); Faberge, 1882; Abercrombie & Fitch, 1892; Chanel, 1909; and more. Hopefully, VS Vincenzo will join this illustrious list one day. Only time and hard work will tell. There's still much left to do.

It's an old adage that with great success comes great responsibility. With TurnKey and VS Vincenzo, the culminations of my lifetime dreams, came the realization that it was time for me to create a legacy of giving to perpetuate my family name. How better to honor my musically gifted father and grandfather than to grant an annual scholarship at my alma mater, Vineland High School in New Jersey, to students who plan to major in music, dance, theater, and fine arts?

I named it "The Professor Enrico Serra & Vincent Spinnato Sr. Scholarship." Winners receive $20,000 over four years, and I travel to Jersey to present them in person. It's been the most rewarding act of my life.

I would also like to make a positive impact on other sufferers of trichotillomania, a lifelong hair-pulling disease brought about by trauma. For me, the trigger was losing my grandmother and the guilt I felt learning that my attempts to perform CPR had actually killed her. My parents sent me to doctors for meds, and when the drugs nearly killed me, to psychiatrists. Even at that young age, while I was dreaming about having my own beauty company one day, I also dreamed of creating a salve or cream—anything—that would help me stop pulling out my hair. The trich was so extreme that my "pulling sessions" sometimes lasted until I was nearly bald. Yet, no matter how much anxiety relief I felt in the moment of pulling, a look in the mirror at my missing hair would send me into major bouts of humiliation and depression.

For me, self-mutilation was extremely ironic because, as you know, I've had a lifelong obsession with my appearance. People have never said (or likely thought), "You need a nose job, an ear job, a tummy tuck, or pec implants." The characteristic that was decidedly disfiguring was my hair, or lack of it.

The trigger to my trich can be any oddball hair that feels a certain way. It can look a little dirty, be covered with hair spray or gel, or appear stiff for any reason. Even a clump of mascara on the eyelash of *someone else* can set off an undeniable urge to pull the offender out. It's not one of trich sufferers' most endearing traits.

Despite the number of potions and lotions on drugstore shelves, there are no *effective* products that make head-and-body hair look and feel a certain way to reduce that overwhelming impulse to pull out hairs one at a time. There's a reason pharmaceutical companies and cosmetic chemists haven't been paying attention. Trich is a hidden disorder, and so few are willing to air their "dirty little secret" that there appears to be no financial gain for pharmaceutical or cosmetic companies to invest in developing a product for it. Experts can't even agree on how many people actually have the condition, because the statistics range from 2.5 to 10 million, hardly an exact figure. However, there are two areas where experts *do* agree. The first is that 80 to 90 percent of trichsters are females, and among the males, a large number seem to be gay. They also agree that onset usually begins at ages nine to thirteen, and is almost always the result of traumatic events.

I know you're wondering, *What's the big deal? Just get help.*

Well, it's friggin' hard. My friend Joanna Locke, cosmetologist, hairdresser to the stars, and trich sufferer, knows how excruciating it is to admit to friends and family that you can't control your impulses. Her desire to hide the condition is so strong that she's never gone to the beauty salon to have her hair done. Instead, she cuts and styles her own hair. This, of course, turned out well for her, because it led to her career.

Unlike people with other disorders that have numerous support groups, trich sufferers who step out of the shadows have only a few options. There is no soft place where they can go for empathy, and no one to talk to who truly understands the daily battle of trying to control their impulses.

Which brings me back to my childhood dream of developing a product to make those offending hairs softer, silkier, and less compelling. Along with the product, Joanna and I have formed a nonprofit organization that we named Tric-Stars, which will hopefully provide a community where people can come out and be counted.

So, how did the collaboration begin?

Joanna and I first met years ago when we were both writing

articles for the same publication. You see, I sometimes write articles for trade magazines and newsletters forecasting the coming trends in the beauty industry. The fun part is writing for high-end consumer magazines I've always devoured, like *Vogue, Vanity Fair, Harper's Bazaar, Esquire,* and *GQ,* where my articles often appear next to ads for my favorite products, like my beloved Louis Vuitton. I'm also a contributing beauty editor for *Modern Luxury Orange County*—me, Vince Spinnato from Vineland, New Jersey, who always yearned for this kind of recognition. The only frustrating part is I can't write about myself. You know, conflict of interest and all that jazz.

Anyway, this particular article I was writing was about a totally nontoxic baby line I was developing for a client, and Joanna's article was about the chemicals in hair-dye colors and the need for more organic products. It was her sister, Julie Locke, who encouraged us to get better acquainted. Julie knew I was working on my documentary and looking for a hairdresser to appear on camera trying to disguise my bald spots. Since Joanna had female clients with trich, Julie thought her sister would be a good fit. I never imagined at that point that Joanna had trich, too.

The friendship was meant to be. I had been to dozens of hairdressers who tried their best, but had no clue how to help camouflage my bald spots. Joanna, on the other hand, was a frickin' genius at disguising them during the many iterations I went through while we were filming.

When she confessed that she had trich, too, I was blown away. She was the first friend I had met with the condition, and I was hers. It was a powerful moment. After decades with no one to talk to, we had finally found another human who truly understood, someone whose shoulder we could cry on and with whom we could be totally open.

No medication or topical product worked for me until a few years ago, when I discovered that doing a combination of waxing my body from neck to nuts and gathering UVB rays in a tanning bed greatly reduced my symptoms.

Yet, not everyone can afford to do either of these practices, which is why Joanna and I are working hard to bring a low-cost product to market quickly. We want to more effectively help fellow trichsters deal with the condition. If the planets are aligned, Tric-Stars will one day help sufferers turn their shame into acceptance. We're working hard to make that happen (https://tric-stars.org).

As for my pursuit of beauty, it's been a hell of a ride. I've morphed from someone so obsessed with exterior beauty that I nearly killed myself seeking perfection, to someone who actually feels comfortable in his own skin. After years of letting others take advantage of my insecurities and need for affection, I've learned that love can't be bought with expensive *stuff*, excessive plastic surgery, or even beauty products that come in jars, bottles, and tubes. Real love, real beauty, and real self-confidence come from within.

I've also come to realize that beauty, like the wild yellow buttercups blooming at Auschwitz, can thrive in the most hostile environments. It is within all of us, just waiting to emerge.

Acknowledgments

Writing this book was much harder than I thought, but more rewarding than I could have ever imagined. **I want to acknowledge and thank all the people who have enriched my life and been true friends through good times and bad.**

None of this would have been possible without my ghostwriter and friend, Mickey Goodman.

Thanks to Tandy Martin for listening and interpreting my stories for many years to provide the outline of stories and events for this book.

To Marilee Davis, "Mama Mar," my dear friend, second mom,

book manager, and publicist, for helping me through the best and worst times of my life and for guiding me daily for many years.

To Marie Ardita, my brilliant, longtime mentor and dear friend, who has helped me hone my skills in the laboratory, cocreated my Vincenzo and Aegean skincare lines, and literally saved my life on multiple occasions. Thanks to her for continuing to impart her vast knowledge.

To Evelyn Kirton, my phenomenal friend who is always there for me, including helping me after my house burned to the ground.

To Joanna Locke, the first trich sufferer I ever met, who became the best friend anyone could ask for. I trust her with my life.

To Julie Locke Casper, for being such a great surrogate sister and mentor in my life, and for bringing us all together.

To Laura Locke Mollon for being such an inspiration to me in life and in business.

To Lisa Locke Furar, who has been a beacon of strength and empowerment to me.

To the entire Locke family, and Papa and Momma Locke, who "adopted" me as their only son, brother, and uncle to their children after my parents passed away.

To Laurel Benton for getting me through tough times professionally and personally during my body-image obsession.

To Stacie Ciancarelli for believing in my bat-crazy ideas while we were still in high school and designing my company logo and fragrance bottle, the same one that identifies my brand today.

To Malissa Chappius Busconi, Cheryl Mays Richter, Kristen

Ingling Hass, Bobby Domenico, Billy Luciano, Debbie Spinelli, Jen Rubenstein Sierra, Tara Buonadonna Scarpa, and all my friends from childhood who supported me through the roughest periods of my life and continue to be great friends today.

To Stan Ojeda and the Ojeda family, the best second family anyone could ever ask for. I would not have survived my early years without them.

To Michael Testa and Dr. Gerald Luongo for mentoring me throughout my wild high school years and who remain in my life today.

To Patricia Philips, my high school guidance counselor, who helped me get into the college of my dreams and knew when it was time for me to pursue other goals.

To Doug Tarkington, my college roommate who put up with me through all the nutty stuff I did, like making and selling cosmetics from our dorm room. He even went on road trips to New York with me when I searched for someone in the beauty industry who would hire me.

To Amy Calvi, one of my first friends in California, for letting me live with her for free until I got on my feet. She supported me through my nonpaying, self-inflicted internship days.

To Eydie Venturo, my guinea pig/product tester, for trying every product I developed and giving me feedback.

To Matt Felker, one of my first friends in California, for supporting my dreams to make it in the beauty industry by designing my first brochure, and who, as an actor and model, posed for publicity shots—all for free.

To Jonathan Salemi, the director of my documentary and a dear friend, for believing in my craft enough to write and produce a movie of my batshit-crazy life during the last six years.

To Dr. Sharyn Hillyer Chan, Dr. Cathearine Jenkins-Hall, and Dr. Bob Ghan, my fabulous therapists who try to put my head on straight. I never would have gotten to this point without their wise counsel.

To Lee Paler, my first cosmetic-chemist mentor, who got me into the lab and taught me all the basic skills I needed to launch TurnKey Beauty, Inc.

To Kandarpa McGinty, who helped me hone my skills in the laboratory.

To Gigi Berklite, who brought me clothing and sundries on night one after my house fire, when everything I owned went up in flames.

To Guy and Kendra Langer, business associates and dear friends who have been with me throughout my career and who also helped get me through the trauma of the fire. Guy, who has been in the beauty industry for the last forty years, helped me understand what chemicals can and cannot do.

To Jeff Lewis, who started a GoFundMe campaign in the aftermath of the fire, which helped me get furnishings and everyday necessities for my new home after I lost everything.

To Pam Nolen and Nolen & Associates, who believed in my vision, created my brand, and made it tangible by developing all the packaging for the Aegean and Vincenzo product lines.

To Fred Rarick, Esq., my loyal, dear friend and attorney, who has believed in me and provided free legal counsel for twenty-five years.

To Jeannine Keckeisen, my now-dear friend who worked with me and educated me in finance for twenty-five years.

To Eduardo Madueno, CEO of operations of my company, VS Vincenzo, who taught me so much about running a business.

To Louise Davy, the first investor in my company and a dear friend.

To Jonathan and Matt for believing in me and investing in my Caviar & Diamond skincare line.

To Sandra Arnold, who saved my job at the time by doing all the damn paperwork for me and keeping my dyslexia a secret.

To Ryan Seaman, an actor and writer who later became my yogi and spiritual advisor.

To Geoff Ross of Living Glitter, longtime friend and interior designer, who helped beautify my new home after the fire.

To Mike Macaluso, who cared for me for two years as I recovered from multiple illnesses and became a dear friend and the brother I never had.

To Rene Walczak, my packaging broker, who helped bring all my clients' projects to market and talked me off the ledge when I needed it most.

To Lisa Sahakian, one of my original California friends, who has been my sounding board and confidante for the last twenty years.

To Raven Cristina Cooper, my closest friend from the Hoffman Institute, who has always come to my aid at times when I needed her most.

To Lilian Garcia and her husband, Christopher Jozeph, who supported me in the darkest hours following my many breakups.

And, to all the individuals I have had the opportunity to lead, be led by, or learn from from afar, I want to say thank you for being the inspiration and foundation for this book.

Lastly, to all my beautiful animals, Rebel, Sable, Fallon, Alexis, and Savannah, for the comfort they have provided in the worst of times and for their unconditional love.

Product-Line Brands, Development/Collaborations, and Celebrity Products

CELEBRITIES

Beatrice DeAlba – DeAlba Haircare
Carol Shaw – LORAC Cosmetics
Christophe – Christophe Haircare
Damone Roberts – AM•PM Skin-Wipe System
Darrell Redleaf – 3-in-1 Skincare System
Dayanara Torres/Miss Universe 1993 – Ethnic Haircare
French Montana – Haircare in Morocco
Gwen Stefani – Lip Colors/Lip Stains
Jennifer Lopez – "Still" Fragrance for Women
Jessica Simpson – "Dessert" Fragrances for Body-Care Line
Kiyah Wright – Muze Haircare
Lilian Garcia – "Surreal Star" Skincare

Lindsay Lohan – Sevin Nyne Self-Tanning
Michael Jordan – "Michael Jordan" Men's Fragrance for Foot Locker
Ole Henriksen – Ole Henriksen Skincare
Orange County Housewives – Energy Drink
Paul Mitchel – Aubio Life Sciences

BRANDS

Alluvia Beauty (Hoffman Estates, IL) – Exclusive 25 SKU bath-and-body line for Kmart/Sears

Annmarie (Berkley, CA) – Wild-Crafted Organic Skincare, Haircare, and Sun Care

Blended Global Skincare (Scottsdale, AZ) – Six essential boosters of serum concentrates that can be used alone or mixed with any product

DayNa Decker (Laguna Beach, CA) – Luxury-scented candles, diffuser, and body-care products

Dermal RX (Los Angeles, CA) – For serious skin conditions: rosacea, eczema, psoriasis, and dermatitis

DeVita Natural Skincare (Phoenix, AZ) – All-natural skincare and personal-care company

Di Lucina Skincare (Sydney, Australia) – Comprehensive skincare system to treat the effects of PMS and menopause

Dream Cream (New York, NY) – Sexual-dysfunction cream for women

Edge Systems (Signal Hill, CA) – Daily essential products for medical use, pre– and post–plastic surgery

Erina Beauty (Tokyo, Japan) – Skincare, haircare, and bath-and-body 120 SKU product line

Evolution Haircare (Venice Beach, CA) – Hair-regrowth program

Forces of Nature (San Francisco, CA) – Medical essential-oil blends to treat herpes, warts, yeast infections, hemorrhoids, scars, and cold sores

InstaNatural (Orlando, FL) – All-natural skincare and personal-care company

Jason Natural Products (Beverly Hills, CA) – 350 SKU packaging change; global translation to Canadian French; developed 15 new SKUs for the Jason Brand

JDP Chemical (Columbus, OH) – Foot heat-protectant spray

Just Love & Sauce (Temecula, CA) – All-in-one sensual pleasure, massage, and moisturizing oils

Kalon (Long Beach, CA) – CBD Prestige skincare line

LBC (Long Beach, CA) – Luxury cannabis lifestyle brands

Lifeline Skincare (Carlsbad, CA) – Stem-cell skincare and personal-care products

Mila Products (Beverly Hills, CA) – Product line based on human placenta

Nutress Hair Care (Kirkland, WA) – Ethnic haircare system

Oona Products (New York, NY) – Herbal supplements to treat PMS and menopause

rmdi (Phoenix, AZ) – Healing skin remedies

SeneGence International (Irvine, CA) – Skincare, bath-and-body, and color-cosmetic line sold as multilevel marketing

Shakalo (Encinitas, CA) – Beach sand-repellant skincare

Starbucks (Seattle, WA) – Lip balms infused with Starbucks coffee flavors

Synergy (Denton, TX) – Exclusively for Sally Beauty Supply for Baby Boomers

Synergy for Women (Denton, TX) – Exclusively for Sally Beauty Supply menopause/progesterone cream, sexual-dysfunction formula, throat-and-bust formula, and varicose-vein treatment

U-Thermic (Sydney, Australia) – Australian skincare products to obtain skin's optimal temperature

Zoen Co. (Long Beach, CA) – CBD product subscription line

PRIVATE-LABEL, WHITE-LABEL, AND RETAIL COMPANIES

7-Eleven; Aegean Skincare; Agera Skin Care; Anagen Rx; Aroma Naturals, Inc.; Ass Wax; Body Drench; Bootie Babe; Boscia; Bright Glow Candle Co.; Brighton Collectibles; Carefree Natural; Catalina Botanicals; Caves Inc.; Central Market; Circle of Friends; Costco; Cost Plus World Market; Elite Candles & Gifts; Face Logic; Forces of Nature; Gap/Banana Republic; Glow Medispa; HEB; Illuminations; JM-Style House; Johnson & Johnson; Kate Somerville; Kerstin Florian; Kmart/Sears; Lash Girl Studies; Longs Drugs; Mama Sol; MarMaxx Group – TJ Maxx/Marshalls; Meijer; Millcreek; Miraceuticals; Pavane; Procter & Gamble; Pure Puppy; ReTress Haircare; ReVive; Rubber Ducky Sunscreen; Safeway; Sally Beauty; Sephora; Seven Oaks Farm; Shades Hair Color; Skin Elements; Skin Nutrition; Swedish Beauty; Tarte Cosmetics; The Limited – Victoria's Secret, Bath & Body Works; The Walt Disney Company; TIGI Haircare; Trader Joe's; Trinity Beauty & Skincare; Tush MD; Uni-Liver; Vincenzo Skincare; Walgreens; Walmart; Wegmans; Wet® lubricated products; Whole Foods; Zodiac Baby

Index